William Black

Stand fast, Craig-Royston!

Vol. I

William Black

Stand fast, Craig-Royston!
Vol. I

ISBN/EAN: 9783337040963

Printed in Europe, USA, Canada, Australia, Japan

Cover: Foto ©ninafisch / pixelio.de

More available books at **www.hansebooks.com**

Mrs. Severn. A Novel

By Mary E. Carter,
Author of 'Juliet'

'SIN COMES TO US FIRST AS A *TRAVELLER;* IF ADMITTED, IT WILL SOON BECOME A *GUEST;* IMPORTUNATE TO RESIDE, AND IF ALLOWED SO FAR, WILL SOON AND FINALLY BECOME *MASTER* OF THE HOUSE'

IN THREE VOLUMES
VOL. II

LONDON: RICHARD BENTLEY & SON, NEW BURLINGTON STREET, PUBLISHERS IN ORDINARY TO HER MAJESTY THE QUEEN

MDCCCLXXXIX

CONTENTS

PART I—*Continued*

CHAPTER XIV
	PAGE
SCILLA AT THE SALE	1

CHAPTER XV
| HOME AGAIN | 23 |

CHAPTER XVI
| 'T' CORP'S AT LAFER HALL' | 43 |

CHAPTER XVII
| 'ONLY THE ADMIRAL' | 58 |

CHAPTER XVIII
| NIGHT AND A GATHERING STORM | 74 |

CHAPTER XIX
| 'SIN THE GUEST' | 98 |

PART II

CHAPTER I
	PAGE
SPRINGTIME	115

CHAPTER II
AN ENCOUNTER ON THE MOOR . . 135

CHAPTER III
CYNTHIA FACES THE SITUATION . . . 150

CHAPTER IV
ANNA FACES THE SITUATION 182

CHAPTER V
AFTER STORM, CALM . . . 201

CHAPTER VI
THE RUBICON IS PASSED . . . 222

CHAPTER VII
THE REPORT OF THE BRIDE 248

CHAPTER VIII
MEETINGS AND A MISS 263

MRS. SEVERN

PART I—*Continued*

CHAPTER XIV

SCILLA AT THE SALE

But of these schemes Scilla must know nothing. She must not even suspect that a scheme might exist. She was that daft, that there was no saying what she might do if she once got an idea that poaching was afloat again. He thought she was even capable of delivering her own husband's father up to justice, if she knew he were once more on the track of dishonest dealing. Nor was he wrong.

As he slowly tidied himself upstairs, he debated over all the possible contingencies that occurred to him. In leaving the kitchen he had glanced at her, and the brooding thoughtfulness of her face struck him as dangerous. Left to herself for the rest of the day after the heat of this discussion, it was more than likely that she might evolve something very like the truth out of her scanty knowledge. Suspect him she must. His ways were evil. If they did not tend to one forbidden object, they must tend to another. She might begin to watch him—yes, even to dog his movements. There was a courage about her which his vocabulary could only qualify with the one word, devilish. He was unacquainted with the ennobling phases of motive which might have suggested to him a finer phraseology.

When he came down again he found the kitchen empty. But the back door was open, and looking out he saw the stable door was too. He crossed the flags that led to it across the little garth of coarse grass which a patched and dilapidated fence, half of ragged bits of wall, half of wooden rail or rusty wire, enclosed for drying clothes or rearing ducks. Scilla was on her knees beside Nobbin, whose hind leg she was rubbing with an embrocation which Hartas did not know they possessed. The old horse was looking round at her, and she, while gently busy, looked back at it. There was a wistful uncertainty in her eyes which was not perhaps wholly lost on the animal any more than it was on Hartas.

'Scilla,' he said, 'it's nobbut a step to Northside Edge, and there are certain to be folks you'll ken. Put on your gear and come away with me.'

As he spoke she slowly transferred her eloquent glance of inquiry to his face. The animal had met it better than did the man. He shuffled uneasily to and fro, shiftiness expressing itself in every gesture. Taking up the brush he slapped Nobbin's flanks as though to assure himself of their substantiality and began dusting them down with a hissing sound.

'Gin you'll gang I can send her home with you if she falls short o' t' distance, you see,' he said, labouring hard at his feint of work.

Scilla got up, re-corking the bottle and shaking her apron free of the hairs that had fallen into it as she rubbed.

'I'll go, but you'll none send her home,' she said.

'Or maybe bring her neither, you think?'

'Maybe not,' said Scilla imperturbably.

Hartas swore at her as she disappeared through the doorway.

'If I'd held my tongue I'd have saved him that oath,' she thought, and urged by this regret she quickened her movements that waiting might not add fuel to his temper, and leave him with less forbearance for any exigency that might occur at the sale.

An hour later they were at Northside Edge.

It was one of the highest class farms of the district, and had been held from father to son during ten generations. But the last tenant had died childless, and his widow was retiring from the congenial labours of a lifetime into dull and aimless gentility in Wonston. It had been a well-furnished house. Independently of the oak delf-racks and tables, and the ancient pewter dishes and tankards that were fixtures and belonged to the Admiral as landlord, there was abundance of good deal and mahogany, which was likely to attract a better class of purchasers than the normal dales farmer, purchasers with longer purses and without rickety shandrydans on which to secure their purchases with the help of faith and rope. This expectation it was which had determined Luke to take his trolly. Its advantages as low-hung and spacious must strike every one who invested in a chest of drawers, a 'sofy,' or a bedstead. He had jumped at Hartas Kendrew's offer. He had a nag at his disposal for getting the trolly to the Edge, but none for getting it away again. That means should be forthcoming for this when it was laden with other folks' property was of course necessary. It was a sharp neighbourly thought of Kendrew's, and strengthened his liking for him as a business-like partner in depredations which might make 'a mint o' money' for both.

The sale proved to be of precisely the character which Luke had anticipated. He was a quiet but observant man, and in the possession of a fund of imagination rare in men of his class, generally found that his calculations agreed pretty closely with his realisations. His covert glance at the scene as he rattled over the ruts of the road in the last field assured him to-day that again he was not far wrong in his expectations. Among the crowd, ceaselessly shifting round the furniture arranged about the auctioneer's table on the flags at the back of the house, or appearing and disappearing now at one window of the dismantled rooms, then at another, there was a goodly sprinkling of gentry, as well as a neat percentage of those dales farmers to whom carts were useless, but who were not of sufficient standing to own 'traps.' He already felt in his pocket the chink of as many shillings as would perhaps change into gold to the tune of a pound or two. The unusual opportunity pleased him. It had an aroma of 'stolen sweets' about it. He was a 'cute un,' was Luke Brockell, and folks must know it and respect him accordingly. Not, however, that that much signified so long as he felt he had good reason for being pleased with himself.

Foremost in the crowd, and always conspicuous from his height, was Mr. Severn. Before Luke jumped off his trolly to unharness he had also caught sight of Admiral Marlowe, but it was to be concluded he was not going to stay long, for at the lower end of the field Miss Marlowe was curveting on horseback, evidently trying to keep warm, while a groom led another horse. Presently she cantered up the slope and drew rein close to Luke, with a smiling bow to a man who had been examining a fine oak chest with critical discretion of eye and touch. It was Canon Tremenheere. He raised himself and went up to her.

'I never imagined you haunted sales,' she said. 'It must be some special attraction. Yes, I see,' as he turned and pointed it out, 'and I admire it very much. It is in character with Sanskrit and Hindostānee and all your other attractions. But what a curious scene this is!'

'So peculatively eager and yet so studiously indifferent. I speak from experience. I long for that chest, but so I believe does

Major Russell. We each mean to outbid the other, but we are absolutely unconcerned as to each other's chance. Only, he knows when I am near it, and I know when he is.'

'Here he comes,' said Cynthia. 'Now what must I say if he asks if I admire it?'

'That is just what he won't do. He will talk of anything but that in my hearing. There is an oak table which he is more likely to laud. It is very nice, has two leaves that let down.'

'But won't hold MS. or old tomes. However, you shall not perjure yourselves with me for an excuse. How do you do, Major? I saw you talking to my grandfather just now. I wish he would be quick and finish his business.'

'Yes, it is not exactly the day to revivify eighty years of age,' said Major Russell. He was a youngish man with a vacant expression and remarkably small features. His growth, physical as well as mental, seemed to have concentrated its efforts on his moustache. This was unusually heavy, and he caressed it unceasingly.

'I call it a beastly nuisance, this sort of thing, all sodden together. The ground is not fit to stand on, and it looks as though heaven would discharge a deluge again at any moment.'

'Very grim and gray,' said Tremenheere; 'we want a Herkomer to put it on canvas.'

'If I stay much longer I am sure I shall be quite melancholy,' said Cynthia.

'With chill, I fear,' said Tremenheere, looking at her anxiously. 'I'll go and see if I can't represent to the Admiral the expediency of going.'

As he turned, Cynthia's horse, restive from the excitement of so many people moving about it, struck out suddenly and scattered the onlookers to a greater distance. She cantered it up and down once or twice, and coming back found herself alone against the trolly near which she had previously stood. But it was no longer empty. A young girl was sitting on the edge; her feet hung crossed in an attitude of weariness, and one hand supported the other elbow on whose hand her cheek rested. She was evidently watching two men who were examining a jaded-looking old horse under the shelter of the hedge at a little distance. They were disputing angrily. Cynthia could almost hear what they said, although their voices were lowered. She looked keenly from them to the girl, wondering if the horse were intended for the trolly, and curious to judge of its condition.

In a few moments one of the men led it forward. It limped painfully, and Luke Brockell from behind gave it a resounding blow with a knotted stick he carried. A low cry from the girl arrested Cynthia's attention for an instant. She glanced down at her and saw how the blood had rushed into her face, and how her eyes gleamed with resentment. She drew up close to her and touched her with her whip.

'Come,' she said, 'they shan't abuse it. I'm sure they mean to harness it into this and they shall not. It is not fit for work.'

Scilla looked up at her. She knew Miss Marlowe. But she had never seen her look as she did now. There was a flash of indignation in the beautiful eyes that were generally radiant with serenity. It seemed to transform her whole face and figure into the natural imperiousness of her position. This imperiousness Cynthia so rarely felt that when she did, she indulged it.

'Listen! Now we hear what they say and I don't want to hear,' she went on before Scilla had time to speak. 'I shall forbid them to use it. They have not seen me yet but they must.'

She touched up her horse, and the next moment had swept across the field and was standing before Hartas and Brockell.

'I forbid you to ill-treat that poor beast!' she exclaimed.

Both had been so absorbed, the one in dragging Nobbin by the halter, the other in watching the action of the stiff leg, that they had neither seen nor heard her coming. To Brockell it was like the descent of an avenging angel. He stared at her, open-mouthed and silent, reflecting who she might be. But Hartas knew her. He too was stunned. He had not imagined that his tug of war with the powers of evil was to take the form of this fair girl. So all the darkness was on his side again, all the blackness in his soul. But he would see if he could not pour some of it into her life yet. He had an old grudge against the Admiral. Well, if Fate would have it that she too should be involved, he would rather wage war against two than one.

It might be easier to reach the Admiral's sensibilities through her. Or if the Admiral dropped off, as he might any day at his age, there would be time to work off his vengeance on her. He saw Nobbin's doom in her every gesture, in the straight poise of her figure, in the tension of the outstretched hand that pointed with her whip. He heard it in the command of her tones whose vibration was that of assurance in further powers. Yes, the law fortified her. It had fortified her grandfather when, as Chairman of the Bench of Magistrates at Wonston, he had consigned Kit to the judge and jury who sent him to prison and hard labour. And had not Scilla warned him?

They were not long alone. Those who had not noticed the two men were quick to notice Miss Marlowe's movements. Soon an interested group gathered. Cynthia, after one or two eager questions which Brockell answered, turned and rode swiftly up to the house. She wanted a magistrate but not her grandfather. She had recognised Kendrew. His sinister look had impressed her. She did not flinch, but she remembered some tale that Anna Hugo repeated at the time of Kit's conviction for manslaughter, about an oath of vengeance that the father had sworn. There was no necessity for the Admiral to embroil himself in this affair and she would not allow him to do so. Her quick dauntless eyes had again perceived Tremenheere in the crowd. He was making his way to her. When he reached her she told him all in a few rapid words. He promised to take the case in hand but would not leave her until he saw the Admiral mounted. Having watched them off the field he turned to the group round Nobbin.

On his way he was joined by Major Russell.

'I watched them bringing the brute along the road while we were talking to Miss Marlowe,' said the Major. 'It's palpably a case for the Humane Society. I wonder they weren't dropped on before getting clear of Wonston.' He wore a pince-nez, and, having now adjusted it, recognised Kendrew.

'Why, they're not Wonston men. It's that old blackguard from the Mires who poached grouse, and whose son shot the Admiral's under-keeper,' he exclaimed, quickening his steps. 'Come, Tremenheere, I'm your man. This horse must be shot or I'll give him six months. He's petitioning for it by bringing her here. He's an old scoundrel. Nothing 'll please me more than to give him another lesson.'

Nobbin had been brought up to the trolly but no attempt was being made to harness her. Scilla still sat there, listless but alert to the expression of every face before her. It was she who replied to Tremenheere's questions.

'She belongs in part to us and in part to another man,' she said. 'No, not him,' indicating Brockell, at whom Tremenheere had looked inquiringly. 'She's a pit-horse, sir, and a good one for that. We belong to the Mires, and my father-in-law, Hartas Kendrew, and Dick and Reuben Chapman, they mine for coals and old Nobbin winds the coil and brings them up. That's not hard work. But I say what you gentlefolks say, she never ought to have been brought here for this job. It's only her leg and that only stiff, but I own it looks a deal worse.'

'Honestly spoken, Mrs. Kendrew,' said Tremenheere. He knew her. He was fond of children and had often stopped to speak to Mrs. Severn's children when she was their nursemaid. Later, he had, by Cynthia's wish and sympathy, visited her at the Mires after Kit's conviction.

'*Looks* worse, my good girl,' said Major Russell contemptuously, '*is* worse, I say. Seems to me you're actionable. She's being used in an unsound condition. Come, we must have her saddle off.'

'There's not a sore on her,' said Scilla warmly. 'She's been that well-treated, sir. Never had but two masters and the pit-men the last twelve years. It's our stable, and I've oft tended her myself. You may rub her all up and down and you'll find no sore. And if we've been stinted for a meal, she never has. She's never had an accident, and it caps me how this leg's come so stiff.'

'The outward frame decays, eh, Tremenheere?' said the Major with a wink which the Canon's face instantly showed he resented. "'Tis what we must all come to, men and beasts alike. "A few more years," et cetera. Take off her saddle, one of you loafing fellows, will you?' he added, turning hastily, as he realised that he was going too far towards profanity in the probable opinion of such a man as Tremenheere.

Hartas obeyed. His hands trembled with rage.

'Now see,' said Scilla again, as the Major

examined Nobbin from ear to flank, 'there's not a hair turned any way and never has been. She's none had blows. The pits are scarce a mile from t' Mires, and just there and back she goes once a day and ofttimes only three times in the week. If she's gone with a hobble, many's the time she's come back without it.'

'The leg is stiff and the limp is there,' said the Major. He had been greatly hindered in his examination by his pince-nez constantly dropping off, his nose not being of dimensions which enabled it to keep steady while he held his head at all angles and distended his eye-balls in vain endeavours to find signs of deliberate ill-usage. Having caught and refixed the glasses half a dozen times to a running accompaniment of impatient exclamations strikingly suggestive of oaths, he now straightened himself with a magisterial inflation of his small form.

'The leg is hopelessly stiffened and the

limp is permanent,' he said. 'Kendrew, you'll have to put her out of the way. And at once too, or we'll give you a month's hard labour.'

Kendrew said nothing. He was dumb with rage. Scilla slipped off the trolly, and coming round to Nobbin caressed her head.

'If she's in pain, sir——'

'She's unfit for work,' said the Major.

'It means a deal to us. Very like we shall have to make her whole vally good.'

'She's of no value.'

'And just against winter too,' murmured Scilla again. 'Still, if she's in pain——'

'Suppose you walk her down into Wonston and see a Vet,' Tremenheere interposed.

'There's justice in that,' said Brockell. 'I've been taken in with her myself, counting upon her for my loads from the sale and finding her nought but this poor old screw that I'd expect the first p'liceman to drop on. But right's right; and she may have got lamed in coming or a bit of a mixture may wear it off. Let a Vet have his say as well as this here gent, as I suppose plumes himself on being a magistrate.'

'Plumes himself! No insolence, my man,' exclaimed the Major.

'Come, come, Russell,' said the Canon in a low voice; 'it will be much better not to show temper here. It's hard lines upon them, after all. Let them keep quiet for an hour, and then you'll be at liberty and can go down with them. Pity but there were a Vet here, you will have to see it through.'

Hartas was reharnessing Nobbin to an accompaniment of jeers and reproaches from Luke, who felt that, as the most aggrieved person, he had the right to say anything. But Hartas would not endure reproach. He turned and glared at Brockell, uttering a savage oath.

'You be——' he said. 'If you'll stand by me in spite o' this, I'll give you an inkling o' sommat that we'll make money by, by just holding wer tongues. I kens a thing or two, Luke, that'll come damned heavy on t' Admiral if this here foreign marriage comes off. I tell thee that's a fact. We'll be even wi' Miss Marlowe——'

Scilla was drawing near. He hastened to change the subject. 'And there's always Mrs. Severn,' he said, leering at her. 'Ay, Scilla, my lass, you and I could tell some tales, couldn't we? *Clo*, that's what Lias Constantine dubs her to Dinah, as I've heard Kit say many a time when he were courting about Old Lafer. And *Clo* she is, *old* Clo, *bad*——'

'Father!' cried Scilla, and sprang forward and clapped her hand over his mouth with such force that a gurgling cry rose in his throat as his head was jerked back.

'Now, Hartas, just you be civil to t' powers that be,' said Luke surlily.

But he exchanged a wink with Kendrew, and Scilla saw it.

CHAPTER XV

HOME AGAIN

Scilla went home alone from Northside Edge. It was too far for her to go into Wonston. Moreover, Hartas would not have allowed her to go. This was no job for a woman.

The fog was down again when she reached the moor, and she had to go carefully as it sometimes thickened so closely that she might have lost the track. Once lost, it would have been difficult to find again. Occasionally there was a sudden shower. Then it cleared for a few moments. But so cheerless were the moors, sodden, gray, with water-courses down every hollow, and mists curling on every ridge as though torn from the heavy skies, that she preferred the fog. She was wet through long before she got home. The fire was out, but she soon kindled it. Of one thing there was never any stint at the Mires, the peat shanty was always well stocked. They had stacked fifty-five sledge-loads of turves this summer. Sometimes Hartas brought over a little coal, slack that was not much better than dirt, and travelled well in a sack thrown over Nobbin's back. This, sprinkled on the smouldering embers, would make a flame. She would have one to-day. At least the house should look cheerful. They could not sell their peats towards the cost of poor old Nobbin, that was certain. But how would they be able to meet this disaster? What would Dick Chapman say? Poor old Nobbin! She could not bear to think of her. She hated herself now for having gone on such an errand. And yet she would have blamed herself had she stayed behind. She had led her most of the way, and over the softest places. She had heard and seen all that had passed. She had pleaded—pleaded, indeed, had it been for herself and Hartas rather than for Nobbin?

When the fire was lit, and she had deftly regulated here the opening, there the closing, of a window or door, to fan it the quicker, she went upstairs and changed her clothes. Her room was beyond Kendrew's and she glanced in as she passed. It struck her as being untidy. He had changed his suit, and the discarded corduroys were tossed down at random. They felt damp too. She gathered them up and took them down. He had been constantly in and out during the morning, and the fog had fallen on them. She threw them on the settle until she had had her tea.

By this time she was determined not to be

miserable, at least for an hour or two. Tears came into her eyes when she looked across at the empty stable, but tears would not re-tenant it. And she had no patience with what was useless. Her natural philosophy was of the character of King David's. So she hung the kettle in the rekkon, placed a little table just in front of the fire, and sat down on the fender with the kitten in her lap, and a round of bread on the toasting-fork.

But she had not sat long when her eye was attracted by something bright on the settle. She had thrown Hartas's clothes there, and it was among them that she caught a gleam of yellow and red for which she could not account. Still she was too inert from weariness and sadness, and too comfortable in the glow of the fire, to trouble to move at once. She would see what it was when the kettle boiled and the tea was 'mashed.'

The fire was blazing cheerily now, illumining the dusk fast gathering in the kitchen, and seeming to mock the sullen gloom beyond the window. In a few minutes the kettle hissed. Then followed a feathery curl of steam. Scilla filled the teapot and got up. She had forgotten the gleam on the settle, but was mindful of the drying of the clothes. She went for the folding-rail from the scullery, and took up Kendrew's jacket. As she did so a book dropped out of one of the pockets. She picked it up and looked at it in amazement. Had it been a note for fifty pounds she could not have been more amazed. Hartas rarely read even a newspaper; as for books, she had never seen more than the Bible, and Wesley's Hymns, and one or two Sunday-school prize-books of her own, in the house.

But this was nothing of that kind. It was in fact a novel, a two-shilling railway edition of Bret Harte's *In the Carquinez Woods*. She had never seen a binding like it. It seemed to blaze in her hands, and yet had she not seen something like it when she lived at Old Lafer? Yes, she remembered suddenly, in a flash of vivid remembrance such as is often accorded to trivial things, how she had once been helping Miss Anna to unpack on her return from a visit to Rocozanne, and had taken a similar book from her travelling-bag. She opened it, expecting to see the name of Anna Hugo on the fly-leaf. But there was no such name, or any name. Yet it could not belong to Hartas Kendrew, and unless Mrs. Severn had left it there when last she was at the Mires, how could it have fallen into his possession?

She sat down to tea with it on the table beside her cup and saucer, and slowly turned it over, leaf by leaf. All at once she saw a pencil-mark, and not only a mark but a letter. It was the letter *L*. A few pages farther, and in larger characters there were two letters, *L* again and *D* beyond it. Yet a little farther, and the full name was scribbled slantwise again and again on the margin of both pages. Scilla read the name. It was *Lucius Danby*. But it conveyed no significance to her. She had never heard it. She read a bit here and there as she drank her tea. And it interested her so much that she forgot everything else.

Suddenly there was a loud rap at the door, followed instantly by the lifting of the latch. She jumped up as the door opened and a man walked in. It was quite dark beyond him, but the firelight fell on his face, and she saw it was Dick Chapman.

They stood and looked at each other. Neither spoke. She could see him well, but it was only by the close scrutiny of his regard that he could distinguish the expression of her face, for the light was behind her.

'*You know*,' said Scilla at last. She suddenly felt herself become nerveless and dropped on to the settle. One hand restlessly smoothed the arm of the settle that was polished with age, and somehow seemed to respond to her clinging fingers.

Chapman laughed. He had come forward a step or two, and was slowly drawing off his comforter. Scilla watched the lengthening of his arm as the loose end slid from waistcoat to neck and dropped.

'*Know!*' he said. 'Ay, I've *seen*. I lay I know more nor you.'

'You cannot, Dick. I went to Northside Edge. Miss Marlowe spoke to me before she went up to father and Luke. I knew what was coming. I knew before we started.'

'Then why did you start?' said Chapman with an oath.

'Ask yourself if I could have hindered father going by not going myself.'

The dignity of her tone and the justice of the question struck home to him. He was silent, but went up to the rocking-chair opposite to her and sat down.

'You weren't there too, really, were you?' she said, withdrawing her meditative gaze from the fire to fix it again on him, when he still offered no explanation.

'I wer never nigh t' Edge, fooling round. I wer i' Wonston, ay, that I wer, just on t' other side o' t' street, when t' trolly came round t' corner with t' party on it, and stopped at t' farrier's. Nay, nay, Scilla, I'll give you your due. I'll own you'd never lend yourself to a mean trick except in hopes o' good coming out of it—as good does sometimes for all the world like a chick out o' an egg as had been set down for addled. But I'll assure you o' one thing. When my eyes lit o' that there party, I could hev dropped.'

'Was Nobbin in the shafts?'

'That she wer, and as odd a lot behind as one 'ud look to see out o' a show. Hartas and Luke Brockell, forced to look thick by their shoulder to shoulder for want o' more space; but Hartas glowering fit to send sparks flying; and blocking their backs, a sofy and a chest, and an assortment o' pots and pans and baskits. Major Russell o' t' Manes wer there first, a lad wer holding his horse at t' farrier's door. And then, just as farrier and Major came out, up comes Canon Tremenheere, him that was sweet on Miss Marlowe. And his trap and horse were that splashed, he must hev thundered down. He's that black, but it's he that has the grand manner. T' Major strutted like a bantam cock. Top over t' moon he was with his job.'

'And what did they do—t' farrier, I mean?' said Scilla breathlessly. 'Major Russell had seen she hadn't a hair turned.'

'Do! He'd had his say with t' farrier. He kenned Hartas for a poacher o' grouse, and I lay there'd been warm words up at t' Edge. Howsomever we'd no chance. Brockell had hallooed at me to join 'em, but I kept mum. I thought I'd hev it out with Hartas later. T' farrier lifted her limb and stroked it, and she wer taken out o' t' trolly and walked up and down. T' Major followed her as though he thought she wer acting t' old soldier, and would sudden fling her heels in t' air and gallop off out o' his reach. But there wer no such luck for us! And when we all saw how she hobbled, Hartas swore—ay, out loud. And Canon Tremenheere, he just leaned ower t' edge o' his trap, and says he, quite gentle, " I'm that sorry, my men." '

'He did!' said Scilla, with a tearful smile. 'Yes, it was him as was good at the Edge too. He gave the chance with the farrier.'

'Well, he's a rare un. But for the justice of it, he'd never hev let us lose her. But I kenned the justice of it. It's my opinion Hartas 'll run his neck into t' noose one o' these days. He was devil-possessed to show her out o' the Mires.'

'Then did you know she was really bad, bad enough for this?' said Scilla slowly. It had not occurred to her before that they had indeed worked her, knowing her to be wholly unfit for work.

'Poor old screw!' said Chapman, with a smile at Scilla's innocent ignorance. He knew of her purchase of the embrocation, and had pitied her folly at the time.

Scilla caught the smile and its significance. She flashed into a moment's passion, clenching her hands at the thought that she had actually petitioned for that worn-out, painful life.

'I hate you cruel men!' she said.

'Ay, I shot her,' said Chapman.

'You did!' Scilla exclaimed, with dilated eyes. She had not been prepared for so quick a climax.

'Ay, I did. Major says to us, "She must be put away, and I'll hev it done at once." We all went down to Bellerby's field by t' side o' t' Navigation, and Luke Brockell knew where to get a gun. He went for it, and when he came back he put it into Kendrew's hands, and he says, says he, quite low, " It's double-barrelled."'

'Yes?' said Scilla, to whom the full meaning of this did not occur.

'Hartas couldn't hold it or dursn't. It seemed to me likeliest he'd not trust himsel, t' Major wer that near. So I took it. And I fired. The first shot killed her. And, Scilla, t' devil wer that hot in me I well-nigh turned it on t' Major. He weren't three yards away. I'd hev shot him dead.'

'Dick!' exclaimed Scilla, turning white with horror.

'But I thought as quick—" They'll hang me!"'

'Thank God you did!' said Scilla. The tears gushed from her eyes, and she threw herself back into the corner of the settle and covered her face with her hands.

There was silence for a little while. Then Chapman leant forward, and taking up the poker, cleared out the ash from the lower bar, and after giving the fire a stirring so vigorous that the white dust covered his hair and beard as though they were floured, deposited it again with a rattle against the fender. By this he meant to infer that Scilla had had long enough for giving vent to her emotions.

She was quick to feel this, and, sitting up, looked at him questioningly.

'Ay,' he said, 'it's a bonny job for you.'

'I know. I told him,' she said, again falling back listlessly.

'If he'd been content to let her bide i' the stable we'd hev had her yet for many a day.'

'She's better gone.'

'That's none the point o' view of us men. I suppose Hartas 'll hev a nice nest-egg that he's been wanting to invest in some new horse-flesh. Well, the sooner the better. The pits 'll be quiet until he does. I'll give him to understand this in t' morning. Half that nag wer mine. And I'll come on him for damages.'

'You can't do that, Dick. *She* was damaged.'

'I'll do something, howsomever,' he muttered. 'Sike a job's fit to turn a man's blood; it is, I say.'

Scilla did not answer. There was not even safety in assent. Contradiction, as leading to argument, would have been safer.

Chapman got up.

'Well,' he said, 'I thought you'd like to hear t' end. Brockell said you were at Northside Edge. You'll have long enough to wait for Hartas, I lay. Indeed it'll maybe be best if he shumbers along o' t' roadside nigh Wonston. The waters were that out when I crossed t' old bridge that they'll most like be over it by midnight. There's been a power o' rain up west.'

'Maybe he won't come that way.'

'Better come that way as by t' pits. As sure's my name's Richard Chapman he'll drop down t' shaft one o' these nights.'

'I don't think so. He doesn't come by them since that time he got to t' shaft; you'll mind it?'

'And swung over it one minute. Ay, I mind. That sobered him a while. But nought 'll sober Hartas Kendrew for good but hell-fire. Well, I thought you'd like to hear t' end o' t' poor old screw. And now I'll wish you good-night.'

'Good-night,' said Scilla.

He opened the door and stepped into the darkness. Scilla stood a moment looking out. It was raining still. The patter of the drops into the rising waters of the marsh was distinctly audible. She waited until she saw the glimmer of light that revealed for an instant the opening of Chapman's door. Then she closed her own, and, stirring the fire, sat down on a little stool before it, with her back against the settle and her hands clasped round her knees.

In this position she very soon dropped asleep.

It was midnight when she suddenly awoke, as though roused by some noise. She started up, bewildered by the darkness, and feeling cramped and chill. As she found the match-box and lit the rushlight, recollection returned, but with it the certainty that a familiar sound had awoke her, that of the closing of the stable-door. A new door had been hung in spring, and the wood, not being well-seasoned, swelled with damp weather, and needed a strong pull before the sneck fell. Hartas must have returned, but why had he gone to the stable?

She opened the back door and stood, shading the light with her hand. Heavy steps were certainly crossing the flagged path of the garth, but they were steady ones. This made it more improbable that it was Hartas.

'Father,' she said.

'It's me,' said Hartas's voice.

She stood aside and he passed her. A glance showed her he was sober. He sat down on the settle and kicked off his boots. Then, taking up the candlestick, he crossed to the stairs. As he reached them he turned and said slowly, 'I've bedded down t' mare and locked t' door. Come away to bed, Scilla.'

'Father!' she said, in a tone of expostulation, for she thought he was either drunk after all, or trying to deceive her. He would not know that Chapman had been in.

In the morning she was down early, for it was Saturday. While she was busy black-leading the grate, Hartas went through into the garth and straight to the stable. She suspended her vigorous brushing to listen to his movements, and was astounded to hear within a few moments the whinnying of a horse. She sprang up and ran to the scullery window. Yes, there it was again, and Hartas was just dipping a pail into the trough at the spring. Excitement turned her faint. Was it Nobbin? Had Chapman been making game of her? Had the farrier thwarted the Major and spared Nobbin? For, if not, how could a horse be there, how could Hartas have paid for another, letting alone have found one in this short time? She thought over Hartas's manner of the night before. It had certainly been unlike what she had expected. She had been prepared for drunkenness, rage, and oaths. Whereas he had shown the self-command of a man who felt himself even with the world, and proof against the spitefulness of adversity.

'Oh! I hope it's Nobbin,' she thought. 'If it isn't, I'll be certain sure he's making money with the snares again, and that that's what he's wanted of Luke Brockell, some one to get the birds away for him.'

But it was not Nobbin. Hartas presently went down to the marsh, she felt sure he was going round to Chapman's. This was her opportunity. She slipped into the stable, and there stood a gray mare. Nobbin had been a bay. This one was of a more sturdy build and in better condition, her hide was sleek, she might be old but she was not worn. She did not look round at her as Nobbin always did, but champed phlegmatically at the armful of freshly-cut rushes in the manger. Scilla had not the heart to make friends with her. She turned away. One thing she would not do, she would not ask Hartas any questions. He would only tell her lies.

CHAPTER XVI

'T' CORP'S AT LAFER HALL'

AFTER this all went on as usual at the Mires. Whatever Chapman might think, he was silent. Soon afterwards the weather changed and frosts set in. The constant probability of a snowstorm sent custom regularly to the pits, for fear that at last it should come and find the home-supply low. Times were good at the Mires. From the ridge above the hollow Scilla often saw a line of six carts traversing the coal-road. Thus the coal was sold as quickly as it was brought to the surface. This helped to keep Hartas sober too, for he was always sober during a run of luck.

Scilla hoped his purchase had been made on credit and that the debt would soon be cleared. Never had her home been quieter or happier. She could sing out of a lightsome heart as she went about her work.

Thus it drew on quickly to Christmas and still there was no snow.

But one day in the middle of December Hartas spoke of a storm gathering. He had been across the moors towards Wherndale, and the West was packed with fleeces.

'They'll be shaking themselves out come another twenty-four hours,' he said. 'If there's any marketing to do for cheer o' t' year, thee'd better trip it quick into Wonston. We'll likely be shut in for a month or two.'

'I've got all we want from the butterman,' said Scilla. 'But there's one journey I'd like to make. Never a Christmas has come but I go and see Miss Anna and the childer, you know. And I met Miss Anna a while back, near the Hall, and she said I was to be sure and go. She's a bit of honey for us.'

'Then gang to-day.'

'And, father, there's this,' Scilla said, going to a drawer in the delf-rack and taking out the book she had found in his pocket on the night of the Northside Edge sale. She had forgotten it, and had only found it that day by chance.

Hartas's dull eyes brightened with one of his chuckling laughs. 'I knew thee had it,' he said. 'I knew thee must hev it. You can give it me here. I hev t' bit o' letter paper I found in it all safe, but in t' book itsel there's one page I'm terrible fond on.'

'Whose is the book?'

'Mistress Severn's, I expect. Leastways I came across it on a hummock where I'd seen her sitting t' afternoon she wer spreeing here last. Ay, ay, Scilla, I ken all about that. I wer crossing t' moor and I saw her; and I saw Dinah Constantine come out o' t' fir-woods and strike across here, and Dick Chapman told me Mr. Borlase drove Miss Anna. What a shindy! Dick wer hanging about t' stable and he saw her himsel, and said she looked desperate-like. I'm fair certain t' book's hers.'

'Then I'll take it back to-day. I've a fancy it's really Miss Anna's.'

'Ay, thee can tak it. This *Lucius Danby* fair caps me, Scilla. See thee!'

He turned at once to a page whose number he had evidently remembered.

'I've seen it,' said Scilla, not troubling to go nearer to examine the writing to which he pointed. 'I don't know why it should, though.'

'But I do,' said Hartas. 'And maybe you will too, one fine day come spring. For that's when it's to be, folks say.'

'When what's to be?'

'Thee'll ken soon enough for t' purposes o' Providence.'

'Well, I think I'll go to Lafer this very day after dinner.'

'You ken Miss Marlowe's going to wed?'

'Yes, I've heard tell of it. She'd have wed afore this if she'd had a mind to.'

'And her man's been stopping at t' Hall and all's fixed.'

'I hope they'll be rare and happy.'

'And his name's Danby, *Danby*, Priscilla.'

'Is it, father?'

'Scilla, there's one gift in which you take after none o' your kind. Even one cow 'll skime over t' hedge at another.'

Scilla laughed. She knew what he meant.

'It's always uncommon wonderful to me,' he said. 'For I lay t' highest leddies in t' land hev a mint o' curiosity, and I allus said thee wer cut out for a leddy, only t' devil ran away wi' t' pattern.'

She laughed again, and was just going into the scullery with an oven-shelf on which a meat-pie had boiled over when he called her back, speaking in a tone which compelled her to obey. In that instant his appearance had changed as completely as the brant from which the thunder-cloud chases the sunshine. A sombre shadow had fallen on his face. From beneath its shaggy brows his eyes glowed like live coals. His hands were clenched. His trembling shook the settle.

'Nay, it's none a fit,' he said as he saw her terrified look. 'Leastways not a fit o' God Almighty's. It's passion, t' devil's own black passion, and one o' these days when t' time's ripe it'll fire me. Priscilla, ye ken who did it, not Luke Brockell or Major Russell or t' farrier. 'Twer Miss Marlowe. Curse her! And 'twer t' Admiral as sent Kit to prison. Curse 'em both for high-handed close-fisted gentry!'

Then he got up and stumbled out of the house, groping as though he were blind.

Scilla scarcely knew how she finished her work. His manner as well as his words were a revelation to her. Rage, then, had only been slumbering. But surely he was powerless to harm either the Admiral or Miss Marlowe. He held no secret of theirs as he did of Mrs. Severn's. But, except as Admiral Marlowe's agent, he had no grudge against Mr. Severn. Surely it was impossible that he should touch Miss Marlowe or influence the influences round her to the slightest misery. While he cursed, would not Heaven bless?

The day was still bright when she started on her walk, but the clouds of which Hartas had spoken were just showing their white shoulders above the ridge of the western moors. Above them the sky was a deep cold blue. The frosty sunshine became each moment frostier, seeming to scintillate in the air before it gemmed the hoar of the stark ling and rushes. Not a breath of wind stirred. The world seemed to lie under a spell of expectation, as the clouds, with imperceptible movement, peered over into its hollows and mouldings and far-sweeping undulations. An hour's fall of flakes would bring all under their domain. How vast, how cold, how dead the whole scene would be looking to-morrow! For a storm was coming. There could be no doubt of that with this hush over all, this rigid dryness in every breath she drew. She was glad to leave the moors behind. Their silence oppressed her. It would even have been a relief had a whiff of breeze rattled the rushes.

It was not so lonely in the plantations. Each trunk and stem had its companion. The sunshine, filtering through, fell softly on a sober tapestry of bramble and ivy and moss. The frost was not so strong. Here and there the ground was damp. But at the bottom the stream trickled between icicle-hung boulders, or gathered in ever-lessening ice-bound pools.

And now the path sloped down to the

bridge and she could see Old Lafer, a gray block against the bare larches.

By this time the sun had gone in. She had known it would not go down to-day. Those masses of cloud would thwart it, however good its intentions might be as to a rosy bed and a warm good-night! But she had not expected to be so soon left in the cold. She must not stay long or the storm would overtake her. But how much she had to say to Miss Anna! And where would she be? Surely not in the parlour with Mrs. Severn; or if she were, surely she would come out that they might have a quiet talk together.

In going up the fields she had been slantwise to the house. When she got over the stile on to the flags, it struck her all at once that all the blinds were down. And hitched by the bridle to a crook in the wall near the front door was a horse which she was certain was Borlase's. This was still more alarming. There were seven windows to the front, and she looked from one to the other, incredulous of the witness of her own eyes. Yes, every blind was drawn, and, but for a line of smoke wavering into the sky, it might have been a deserted house. Some one, then, was dead. Who could it be?

She got round to the back door without a sound reaching her. Not even the bark of a dog broke the stillness. As she passed the kitchen window she saw Dinah busy at the table. Dinah caught sight of her, and looked up and nodded.

'Come your ways in,' she shouted. 'Nay, there's no call to look that scared,' she went on as she saw her look of breathless inquiry. 'Sit you down and take off your shawl. You'll hev come to see Miss Anna. But you'll none do that to-day. Borlase is here, and she's to gang to Lafer Hall, to keep Miss Cynthy company. Madam's coach is coming to take her off. She's gathering her duds together now, and arguing wi' t' Missis,

I expect. Nay, nay, we've no corp here, thank the Lord, for all the sight o' sike a mum front ud give you a turn. But it's been that sudden, I only saw t' winding-sheet i' t' candle last night, and this morn he's gone. The Master had never a last word with him; but for the matter o' that, his own wife hadn't. The corp's at Lafer Hall, Priscilla Kendrew. Old Admiral Marlowe's gathered to his fore-elders, and none afore t' time, as no one can bring up against Providence.'

'Then Miss Marlowe 'll be mistress?'

'I lay she will,' said Dinah, noisily clearing the bars of turf and ash, and sending a shower of sparks up the gaping chimney, with a final vigorous descent of the poker upon the turves. 'Old Madam 'll none count where all these acres and bags o' money at t' rent-takings go,' she went on, as she returned to her baking-board and the thuds of the rolling-pin on the paste. 'It'll be the young blood that'll come in. A pity it is that t' old lover cannot come in too. But they'll have to bide a bit now afore they wed, and biding's none good for courtings. God A'mighty only kens what may come of it. This death may be a makeshift o' His; maybe He's repented o' t' footing another man's got with her. And he an alien; ay, it's against nature! It riles one like. I ken it does our Master, he's none taken wi' this Mr. Danby. I've heard him say times over, t' Canon is the man for her. But she wer certain sure to go right against what her own folk mapped out so plain. If they'd talked against him, she'd have taken to him. If I'd talked praise o' Kit Kendrew, you'd have found out he'd faults, and never have come to this pass, Priscilla. Howsomever, it's Christmas time, and peace and good-will, let us all bide in.'

'That's after you've had your say, not afore,' said Scilla, with a waifish little smile.

'I'll no deny it,' said Dinah. 'The tongue's

a cumbersome member when wholesome truths weight it. They're like one o' them lozenges that stick to t' top o' the mouth, or daze your teeth; suck, suck as you will, either you're stalled o' them, or out they must come. And it's my steadfast opinion that what this mucky world stands most i' need of for a besom is wholesome truths. Nought else 'll sweeten it.'

'But it wer t' truth that hied me on to Kit by your own showing, Dinah.'

Dinah banged the oven door after having inserted her hand to feel its temperature, preparatory to pushing in a shelf of mince-pies.

'There's no arguing wi' some folk,' she said testily. 'They're that set agen any turn o' speech but their own. You'd make a pretty stripe in a tick, Priscilla, that straight and thin must sayings be drawn for you. How-somever, bickerings ain't seemly at this time o' year, and t' childer making a text up i' t' nursery this minute. We'll leave wersels and think o' poor old Madam struck a widow at t' ninth hour, and Miss Marlowe wi' her lording come afore her bridal. A deal better it had ha' been for her man if it had come after; reins and whip I lay she'll hold 'em both. And Lias says so too! Look at wer Missis! She's that fond she rules 'em all to give way to her. I've none patience to go nigh hand her. One i' one way, one i' t' other, it comes to t' same thing; not but what I'd be sorry to name any decent woman in the same breath wi' her. But there, she fair turns me sour! You shall see t' childer, Scilla; just bide here till t' coach has been. Borlase 'll manage Miss Anna, and she'll manage t' Missis. They'll do without you and me. And thank the Lord we've a reasonable excuse for keeping clear o' t' muddle, since we're none asked for. "Clo 'll cut up rough at being left alone," said Lias, when t' doctor telled him his errand. "Clo may," says I, but I made up my mind I'd none fill t' gap. 'Tis lucky for Miss Anna she has t' doctor, bless her! And as for t' other maid, well, better hev Mr. Danby nigh at hand as no one. Ay, he's there again, come for Christmas. He didn't count on a corp and a burying wi' t' mistletoe.'

The oven was ready now, and Dinah's temper cooled over the quiet process of watching the baking. Mr. Severn 'was rare and bigoted' of mince-pies, and they must be done to a turn in spite of her mental distractions over what had happened, and what would happen at Lafer Hall where the good old Admiral lay dead.

CHAPTER XVII

'ONLY THE ADMIRAL'

DANBY had only arrived at Lafer the previous day. It was his second visit, and they were all on friendly terms. They were breakfasting the following morning when the Admiral suddenly fell back in his chair with an inarticulate groan. Cynthia rushed to him, terrified by the frightful flush on his face. Already he was speechless. With the instinct of desperation she dragged the chair from under him, supporting his head on her breast, and with Danby's help laid him flat. They were horrified by his heavy breathing. Danby rang the bell violently for the butler, who had just left the room for the letter-bag. They lifted him on to a couch, and presently Borlase came. He could do nothing. There was no return of consciousness. But she did not leave him until Danby drew her away with the whisper that she could do no more for him.

Then came thought for others; her grandmother, whose frail life might be quenched by such a blow. Every one thought of Mrs. Marlowe, but they thought of Cynthia too, while she would not have thought of herself. Borlase was astounded by the rapidity with which she rallied from the shock. He did not like her tearless self-possession. He wished her to relegate business to Tremenheere and Danby and Mrs. Hennifer. It was unnatural that she should give orders as though she had known emergencies all her life. She might be strong, but she was highly-strung. She would lie awake at nights, become unnerved and break down. All this he represented to Danby, and to herself. But she was convinced that she was equal to the strain, and only promised to yield should she feel it necessary to do so. She would not allow Mrs. Hennifer to be distracted in her attendance upon Mrs. Marlowe. She asked Tremenheere to help her with all arrangements; he was an executor, and the Admiral had long ago given him a sealed letter of instructions. Danby felt himself in the way, and proposed to move to Wonston, to the 'Marlowe Arms,' and she assented. But he would not go until he knew she would have companionship. Some one must be with her to whom she could talk freely, and who would save her from the terrors of imagination, and a probable violent reaction. He named his wish to Tremenheere and Borlase when they were in the library together. Tremenheere eagerly acquiesced.

'But who is there?' he said. 'Of course she must have some one before nightfall. But it is not every one who would do. My sister Mrs. Kerr might, but she's hundreds of miles away. She has not many friends, plenty of visiting acquaintances, but not friends; the young were always too young for her, accustomed as she is to the old. There's Lady Lavinia at the Manes, and Mrs. Ponsonby in the Close, but Lady Lavinia has her house full, and Mrs. Ponsonby's not strong enough, it would impose too much on her to get her to stay at Lafer—stay, that's what you mean, eh Danby? We want some one who'll sleep with her; some capable, sympathetic creature. Who is there, do you think, Borlase?'

Borlase's thoughts were full of one such woman.

'There's Miss Hugo,' he said diffidently.

'Anna,' said the Canon, his face lighting up. 'Exactly. You don't know her, Danby, wife's sister of Severn, the agent; you would see him before. I assure you she's the very person. Cynthia and she are friends, and she would come. Severn will spare her, I know.'

'I'm going in that direction, and I'll ask her,' said Borlase.

'I don't know Miss Hugo,' said Danby. 'But Miss Marlowe has spoken of her——'

'No need to name you,' said Tremenheere. 'Borlase will make it all right. He has more influence there than any one. Miss Hugo is his promised wife.'

'So I have understood. If she would come, I should be most grateful. We might ask Severn, he's in the office.'

'No need,' said Tremenheere again, with a wave of the hand. 'Borlase will send her, and you can prepare Miss Marlowe. A most happy thought, Borlase. They will talk to each other; and Severn and I shall do our utmost to keep business away from them.'

When Danby sent for Borlase he also sent for Mr. Severn. His messenger reached Old Lafer before Mrs. Severn was down.

Mr. Severn was looking through some papers in his secretaire when Danby's note was given to him. Jumping up, he went into the hall, calling for Anna. Anna ran downstairs in time to help him into his overcoat and receive his instructions. He feared matters were serious, he might be detained for long; he would send word how he found the Admiral. On the doorstep he turned, struck by an after-thought. Anna was half-way down the passage to the kitchen, and he did what he had not meant to do, he raised his voice.

'Don't tell Clothilde,' he said. 'She has a morbid horror of illness and death. It may not be fatal.'

Then he pulled the door to.

Simultaneously with the closing of the door, Anna heard her name called. She looked up and there was Clothilde. She was standing at the turning of the stairs, grasping the banisters with both hands. Anna rushed back to her, conscious that she had heard. As she reached her Mrs. Severn turned slowly and looked at her with eyes dilated with terror, and a strange gleam of defiant appeal.

'Who is it?' she said in a strained voice. 'Not *him?*'

'Yes,' said Anna. 'The Admiral. But we don't know much, he may recover. It may be nothing of consequence. Are you ready to come down, dearest?'

'The Admiral!' said Mrs. Severn.

'Yes. The note was from Mr. Danby; he was to arrive last night for Christmas, you know.'

'The Admiral!' Mrs. Severn said again. Her tone was so lightened with relief that Anna looked at her with surprise.

But her thoughts did not seem sufficiently collected to allow her to observe anything, and Anna was finding that she required support. She took her into the parlour, and with her arm still round her waist drew a chair up to the fire. At that moment Mrs. Severn suddenly regained the use of all her faculties, and, straightening her figure, released herself from Anna's help, pushed the chair aside, and walked to the window.

'I think it is most absurd to make such a fuss over trifles. He's quite an old man,' she said.

'Trifles!' said Anna. She was urged to warmth by a presentiment that the worst was to happen at Lafer Hall, and by a smarting suspicion that in some way or other, though how she could not conceive, Clothilde had duped her. 'How can you talk of the Admiral's possible death as a trifle? It won't affect you and me, but think of Mrs. Marlowe and Cynthia.'

'It would probably kill Mrs. Marlowe. Old people must die, Anna. Then Cynthia won't have much to regret. Her reign will begin. She'll be Lady of the Manor before she marries. It'll be an absurd match for her, this. What is Lucius Danby but a returned colonist? Certainly India is our patrician colony; where it does go in for trade it makes merchants, not storekeepers; but he is only a civilian of some kind or other. She ought to marry above that, even Canon Tremenheere would be infinitely more suitable; and there was the Earl—oh! she'll see the absurdity of it now. She'll throw him over.'

Anna had followed her to the window. She felt an uneasy instinctive impulse to look closely at her.

'Clothilde, did you mean the Admiral when you said *him, is it him?*' she said.

'I meant the Admiral. Who else? It was the shock,' said Mrs. Severn. She stooped as she spoke, and, taking up a foot-stool against which she had been tapping her foot, returned to the fire.

There was silence.

Anna stood motionless, leaning against the casement looking out. How frost-bound, hard, and cold the world seemed! It laid a vice-like grip on her heart, straitening, chilling, and cramping her energies of mind and body. Was it the glimpse of the path through the woods to Lafer Hall, which the leafless trees gave, that fascinated her with the expectation of momentarily seeing another messenger emerge on the bridge; or was it Clothilde?

Yet how could it be Clothilde? Why should Clothilde tell a lie, for whom? But she was convinced that there had been a tear on her cheek, and she never wept but for herself. It was to hide its starting to her eyes that she had gone to the window; it was to shake it from her cheek that she had stooped. So she had emotions and stratagems! What was affecting her? By her own confession she cared nothing for the sorrow and loss the Admiral's death would cause at Lafer Hall. It was unlike her, too, to show such interest in any one as she had done in Cynthia. It could not matter to her whom she married.

While she stood, her thoughts becoming more and more hazy and speculative, the neutral tint of the landscape was suddenly accented by three crows that flew out of the wood. Her gaze followed them. She would not have been the half dales girl she was had she not at least remembered what they would mean to Dinah or Elias, if they saw them. For a few seconds they circled above the pastures, then swooped heavily on to the wall that bounded the garden. She looked at them and they at her.

'He is dead, I suppose,' she said.

'*Dead!*' said Mrs. Severn. 'It's a hideous word, Anna; I never have seen any one dead, and I never will. If it's the Admiral, there will be a great funeral; John will be in a fuss. I should not wonder if he wants the blinds drawn down here; but I won't have them drawn. I won't sit in a darkened room, and I won't wear crape. You must all clearly understand I won't have the blinds drawn down; I should scream, I should always be seeing ghosts. John was quite right, I have a horror of death.'

'He said a morbid horror,' said Anna, smiling.

'Well, truer still.'

'Yes, but with less excuse. You might overcome it. Clothilde,' she added, turning and looking at her, 'the moment his messenger comes, whether he sends such instructions or not, I shall draw down every blind to the front of the house. Not that I think it matters one bit, or makes one pin of difference, or adds at all to the sorrow one will feel; but as a sign of sympathy and respect, it must be done. It's a way the world has invented of showing respect, and it shall not be overlooked. As for the crape, no one wears it now; we women are not muffled and benumbed into outward humbugs as we used to be. Where we are humbugs it's in the heart.'

'I, for instance,' said Mrs. Severn angrily. 'And all this cant from you, who informs every one that you don't care for the world, or what it thinks or does.'

'I don't,' said Anna with extreme bluntness. 'Right is might, but sometimes I feel the world's right, sometimes that I am. Then I can stand against the world and not care if I am misjudged. Thus I can also stand against you.'

With this she almost ran out of the room, not trusting herself to hear or say more. There were times now, they had increased greatly of late, when she felt that she could not love Clothilde. She had changed strangely. Her indifference now alternated with irritability and unnatural spasms of liveliness. There was no depending upon what she would do. Her present whims were of an active nature; she went out constantly, and often walked; she would drive into Wonston, and offer to shop or market for Anna; she paid a few calls, and when these visits were returned, came into the room and was fascinating.

At first Anna attributed all to a wish to reconcile herself to the prospect of losing her; being companionable to her children, and gaining an experience of domestic matters that should make her independent of Dinah.

But she was soon undeceived. One day she told her Borlase had asked her to be married in spring. She was met by an outburst of indignant reproaches for ingratitude, and an attempt with passionate tears to make her promise not to leave Old Lafer until Antoinette was grown up. Anna's unselfish nature was deeply stirred. She could not attribute it to pure selfishness on

Clothilde's part. She pondered over it deeply. It generated the terror that she was distrustful of herself and clung to her as the ever-present salvation. The possibility that she should again degrade herself forced the blood to Anna's cheeks and resentful tears to her eyes. That Clothilde, so beautiful, the idol of her husband's heart in spite of all her faults and failings, should become debased, was an intolerable thought. It roused in her so strong a chivalry of womanhood, so ardent a longing to fight evil and grapple every avenue of temptation, so keen a sense of the nobility of duty overcoming inclination, that there were moments when she was on the verge of giving the desired promise.

But so far love for Borlase had held her back from this. It was impossible to give a second promise that should annul a first. The first implied inclination that also involved duty. To reverse this in Clothilde's favour would be a dishonour as well as a grief. She could have borne to suffer, but she could not bear to think that Borlase would, since he had asked her for the right to be her first consideration.

CHAPTER XVIII

NIGHT AND A GATHERING STORM

When Mr. Severn's messenger came from the Hall, Anna drew down the blinds. Mrs. Severn said nothing, but went up to the nursery, which was to the back of the house. Anna joined her after dinner, and they were talking over the necessary black dresses when Borlase's voice was heard in the hall. He had got into the habit of hitching his horse's bridle to a crook in the wall near the front door, and of rapping with the knob of his whip as he entered. When he discovered where the family was, he came upstairs three steps at a time.

Anna met him on the landing.

'Oh, Geoff, how is Miss Marlowe?' she said. Her eyes' sparkle of delight at seeing him was shadowed by thought of the sad home from which he had come. He felt that he loved the shadow even better than the sparkle. He was one of those rare men whose consideration for others makes them unexacting for themselves. It was enough that Anna had confessed her love, the equivalent of their already being one. He could have doubted her as little as himself. He liked her matter-of-fact ways with himself and her interest in others.

'She is wonderful,' he said. 'I fancy she is going to astonish us all, especially the men of law. But we fear a reaction, and we want company for her until after the funeral or Mrs. Kerr can get here. Dear, you won't mind going to her, will you?'

'Of course not,' said Anna. Then struck by a sudden reflection she added, 'But does she want me? Will she care to have me?'

'I am certain of it. You have always been friends, and it is Tremenheere's wish too. That will rule, even though she may trust her own strength. Now go and prepare—this dark gray dress, nothing can be better. And I'll tell Mrs. Severn.'

Anna had not been five minutes in her room when Mrs. Severn came in. She closed the door and walked up to the dressing-table. Her handkerchief was pressed to her face, and she was sobbing.

'Anna,' she said incoherently, 'you must not go. You shall not leave me. John mayn't be home to-night, and I dare not sleep without you.'

'I must go, dear,' said Anna. 'It isn't only Geoff's wish, but the Canon's. And just think that there is no one to look after Cynthia——'

'No one? Every one, you might say.

Yes, every one will be thinking of her, and Mr. Danby is there, what more can she want?'

'A woman, Clothilde. Mrs. Hennifer will have to devote herself to Mrs. Marlowe. Why need you be nervous? It will soon be dusk, and when the lamps are lit you'll forget the house looked dull. Besides, Dad is sure to get home to-night, especially as I shall be away.'

'But it'll be late, and I shall sit listening and getting more and more miserable. Don't go, Anna, for Heaven's sake.'

'There is the coach,' said Anna, as the dogs barked. 'Now be reasonable and unselfish. You might as well be so, for I shall go.'

'Unselfish! Are you unselfish? You would not go unless you wished to go. It's very dull here. There'll be a pleasant excitement there. Mr. Danby, the Canon, Geoffry, all going and coming. Have you not thought that Cynthia 'll find you in the way?'

'Nonsense, Clothilde! Mr. Danby is going down to the "Marlowe Arms." If I stayed, what excuse could I send but that you were hysterical and cowardly? I'll tell Netta and Emmeline not to leave you.'

'As though I were a child!' said Mrs. Severn. She rolled her wet handkerchief into a ball and clenched her hands over it, driving the blood from them until the tracery of delicate blue veins was distinctly visible. Two bright spots burnt on her cheeks. Her eyes, lustrous with tears, were passionate and glowing, as though rain had burst from a sultry cloud as prelude to a storm. She stood, drawn to her full height, her head poised defiantly upon her lovely throat that rose with cameo-like severity of outline from the black edge of her dress. Behind her was the dark oak wainscot. Against it she might have been an ivory medallion but for the glow of feeling tha vivified her face.

Suddenly she went to the window and peered round the edge of the blind.

'John said it would snow to-night. Do you think it will?' she said.

'Yes, I am certain of it. Elias saw a flock of wild geese last night.'

'I shall have to do the shopping now.'

'Of course you will. You will have plenty to do.'

'But if a heavy fall comes, I shall not get out.'

'They'll soon send the snow-plough up to Old Lafer. Do you remember it last year with a team of six horses and two postillions and a fresh pair of horses at every farm-house?'

'It will be very cold,' said Mrs. Severn listlessly. She dropped into a chair, then got up again and fingered some photographs that were on the mantelpiece.

'You'll be sure to see Mr. Danby,' she

said. 'I did think Cynthia would have brought him to introduce to us this time. I should like to see his photograph. You must describe him to me, Anna. Oh, you'll have plenty to tell me when you get home. And I'll do the shopping. The children want their hair cutting too, so it can be done when they're fitted on. Yes, the usual simple blouse they shall have with tucked skirts and crimson sashes and black velvet hoods lined with crimson. Quite sufficient mourning, and very uncommon. That's what I like. My children never are like other people's children. But then you see they are unusually handsome to begin with. Yes, *dear* children! Now, are you ready? Have you got all, your muff and keys and purse?'

'Keys,' said Anna, feeling in her pocket; 'here are the house-keys, I have not time to see Dinah. Don't trouble to come down, dear; go back to the nursery and I'll tell them to draw the curtains early.'

Borlase had gone downstairs and was standing on the steps, flicking his gaiters with his whip and looking impatiently back over his shoulder. He tucked Anna warmly into the coach, the footman sprang to the box, the coachman touched up his horses whose hoofs rang on the flags, there was a splash as they rolled through the runnel from the dairy. Elias clashed the gate behind them and Anna was whirled off across the bleak wintry landscape. Borlase followed as far as the cross-roads beyond East Lafer when the coach turned into the lane leading to the old bridge in the valley. There they waved their hands to each other. Their ways parted. It seemed to Borlase that twilight fell at once after that; he missed the sunbeams of her glance.

But it was still bright in the nursery at Old Lafer, and Mrs. Severn had returned there. The windows faced west, and daylight lingered above the edge of the moors.

Here Scilla came presently to see the children. Her talk with Dinah had been funereal, the 'corp' having given way to the 'burying,' which Elias said was expected to be 'terrible big.' He remembered the burying of the Admiral's father, when the tenantry lined each side of the road from Lafer Hall to Wonston. It was a relief to Scilla when she could go to the nursery. She left her basket downstairs and gave the book into Dinah's charge for Anna, saying nothing about it and knowing Dinah could not read. Dinah knew where the honey was and promised to pack it for her, and she was to have tea before going home again.

When she opened the nursery door, the children, busy with their text, rubbed their gummy fingers on their pinafores and rushed to her. Mrs. Severn was sitting in a low chair near the fire, rocking the cradle and gazing out of the window. She did not speak, but she smiled the smile that was

NIGHT AND A GATHERING STORM

always a marvel to Scilla, it was so subtly sweet in its slowness. Once she remarked upon it to Dinah.

'To see it you'd think she wer a good woman,' she said.

'Ay, you would,' said Dinah. 'It fair maddled me at first. But when I got to ken her, I got to fix its seasons. Either she's none giving you a thought or she wants something out o' you. Lias says it's gall, none honey, and it's rare a man's so set against a well-favoured woman.'

But before she went Mrs. Severn asked her to look at the baby.

'I wish it were yours, Prissy,' she said. She always called her 'Prissy,' to Scilla's vexation; she might as well call her *Pussy* at once! One day she had begged her not to use it; since when she had been more particular to do so.

'If it came to it, you'd none bide to give it up, little darling!' said Scilla, kneeling by the cradle and softly kissing the downy cheeks and tiny fingers.

'Oh yes! It would be better off with you than with me, too.'

'But your own little un; it ud be a bit o' yourself to lose!'

'I didn't want it. *One too many*, I've called them all in turn.'

'You'd have wanted them if they'd not been sent; oh yes, you would, if God hadn't thought of you.'

'God!' said Mrs. Severn, with a low laugh. 'God might make nature, but now it takes its own course, Prissy. If I thought He could help us, I might pray now and then, but we can only be as we are made, some one way, some another."

'Sike talk!' Scilla exclaimed, 'as if we couldn't make ourselves good or keep ourselves bad. I believe God *is* in things, and I'll pray as long as I've breath in my body.'

'That's what Anna says,' said Emmeline.

She was behind them and had not returned to the text with the others. Scilla started, colouring with vexation that they had been overheard. Mrs. Severn looked round angrily.

'Go to your play, Emmeline,' she said. 'How dare you listen or speak? If it had been Antoinette she would never have let us know she was there.'

'Then Miss Emmy's the honestest of the two,' said Scilla as she got up. Mrs. Severn's argument was like a drugged dose, in her opinion.

'We're both honest,' said Emmeline. 'Only Netta thinks to herself and I talk. I'm certain Netta's honest. If she wasn't, Anna would set to work hard and make her be.'

'Anna can do wonders, we all know that,' said Mrs. Severn, and she did not speak again to Scilla.

All was bright downstairs when they went

to tea. A blazing fire flashed along the mouldings of the wainscot. The table gleamed in the lamplight. The chatter of the children drowned the sough of the wind through the passages and in the casement. There was no suggestion of death or tempest. But when Dinah came to clear away she said Elias had stamped snow from his boots at the back door.

'It's rare and thick too,' she said. 'Master 'll none travel to-night.'

Mrs. Severn looked quickly up at her, uncertain whether this were spite. But Dinah seemed imperturbable.

'Light my fire,' said Mrs. Severn peremptorily.

'We shall sit up waiting for your father until ten o'clock,' she said to Antoinette when Dinah was gone. 'And then if he has not come we will go to bed. You will sleep with me, Netta.'

'Emmeline can't bear to be alone,' said

Antoinette, in answer to an imploring glance from Emmeline.

'She will have to bear it,' said Mrs. Severn distinctly.

'Oh, mother, do let me sleep on the settee by you,' said Emmeline with imploring earnestness of tone and gesture.

'Nonsense! You would roll off and awake me. What is there to be afraid of?'

'Ever since she awoke and the moonlight made that shape at the foot of the bed she has been afraid,' said Antoinette.

'Anna said it was only the moon, but I thought——'

'Hush!' said Mrs. Severn, 'it was the moon; Dinah must draw your curtain close, and you must not give way to fancies.'

'But you're afraid, aren't you, mother?' said Jack. He was lolling against the arms of her chair, waiting to wish good-night, and suddenly faced round upon her.

'And what do you think I should be afraid of?' she said.

'Then why won't you be alone?'

'Oh! because I have to sit up for your father, and Anna said I was to have company. Then if Netta went to bed to Emmeline, she would awake her and that would be a pity.'

'It's a lie,' said Jack; 'a big wopping lie, and I'll tell you why, because Emmeline wouldn't be asleep, would——?'

He was stopped by a box on the ear that nearly upset him. Before he had time to recover himself he had had one on the other ear. Mrs. Severn was sitting up straight, a blaze of wrath in her eyes and flaming colour in her cheeks. Astonishment at this new aspect of his mother's made him burst into a howl of tears. They were all astonished. Antoinette, Emmeline, and Joan gazed wide-eyed. Then, as the slaps continued, Emmeline rushed forward, dragged him away and pulled him to the door. Another moment and they were standing in the passage, sobbing in each other's arms.

The passage was dark. The night was so dark that the oblong of glass above the front door scarcely showed even as a light patch. The kitchen door was closed, and Peggy, kneeling before the fire tubbing baby, concealed the usual twinkle of light beneath it. But the darkness was nothing to the children until their sobs ceased. 'I'll sleep with you, Em,' said Jack. 'She *is* frightened, that's why she won't believe you are——'

He was looking at her. He felt rather than saw her, but her eyes were dilating. She was staring up the stairs. Her hold of him became a clutch. Suddenly she gave a piercing scream and fell against him.

Her scream was answered by Antoinette, strung up to respond to any excitement. Mrs. Severn, who had lain down on the sofa with a novel, sprang to her feet, then fell back with her hand to her heart. It was Joan who opened the door.

Peggy was already in the passage, but she was cumbered by baby whom she had swathed in a flannel, and was holding a candle perilously near every one's clothes.

'Where's Dinah?' said Jack. He had been knocked over, but was now on his feet again.

'She's milking,' said Peggy. 'What's the matter? 'Twer a skirl that changed my blood. *A bogy*, thought I.'

'Will you hush?' said Antoinette, glancing fearfully round. 'Something's taken Emmeline, she's in a faint. Jack, help me to drag her into here. Peggy, go back, baby 'll get cold, and just shout for Dinah across the yard, but don't take baby into the draught. Mother, *will* you come and look at Emmeline?'

The childish tone of perplexity, goaded into imperiousness, startled Mrs. Severn into instant obedience. She shuddered, but she drew near and glanced at the white face, then fumbled at the buttons of the dress to give her air.

'It's a faint, but still there were three crows on the wall. What did she see?' she said, almost inaudibly.

'Close the door and ring the bell,' said Antoinette with intense self-repression. 'Peggy must bring vinegar and a feather, and the eau-de-cologne from upstairs. Mother, *will you* nurse baby? Oh, Emmeline darling!' she said, dropping on her knees beside her.

But it was Dinah who bustled in. Without saying a word she took Emmeline in her arms and carried her upstairs. The children followed her. When Emmeline came round she was lying on pillows before the nursery fire, and Dinah's cheery face was smiling at her.

Mrs. Severn was left alone. She dare not go upstairs because of Dinah's anger when she should know the whole story. She scarcely dared remain where she was. She stood upon the hearth-rug, turning to glance first into one corner, then into another, afraid to sit down lest she should be frozen into motionlessness by some touch or appearance. In spite of the ruddy glow around, a spectral something might show itself. She felt as though all the dead Marlowes who used to live and carouse at Old Lafer were afloat to-night. They would sport with an arrant coward, and such she was; yes, the shiver down her back-bone and in her very marrow assured her of the fact. What a fool she had been to push her tyranny over the children so far! Now Dinah would make her own arrangements for their sleeping, and probably leave her alone. But she dare not sleep alone to-night. She was not a woman to scream, but she might die of paralysing fear as she lay in bed. It was bad enough to be alone all the evening. *Until ten o'clock* she had said, and she knew Dinah would keep her to the vigil. It was a late hour for Old Lafer, where the whole household in winter was generally in bed by nine. Only two hours from midnight. She would not be asleep at midnight! She remembered the chills and heats and breathlessness she had suffered from creaking boards, streaks of moonlight, rats, and the ticking of the staircase clock, on ordinary nights. But to-night she would be compelled to listen—not only for ghosts, but for Mr. Severn, who might lose his way in the snow, and rap everybody up late, or even in the early morning.

She got up and went to the window to look out. There should have been a moon, but it was obscured by the storm. By pressing her face to the glass she could distinguish the steady fall of flakes. There was no doubt the snow would soon be thick. All was very quiet; there was no wind. But Mr. Severn would not venture to cross the park and come through the woods, he would have to ride round, and in another hour or two the travelling would be sufficiently heavy to give him a long journey. Probably Elias would sit up half the night. He might. No one could expect her to do so.

She went back to the sofa, and lying down, ventured to close her eyes and think.

So Mr. Danby had arrived at the Hall, and was now relegated to the 'Marlowe Arms.' What did that mean? Oh, Miss Marlowe would never marry him, of course not! Probably she had already repented, and was only too glad to begin at once to show him it was so. She would realise her position now. And since he was in Wonston, *she* would surely see him. How she was longing to see him! The blood rushed to her face at the thought, a smile trembled on her lips. They put up at the 'Arms' when they drove into Wonston; she was to go at once to shop, she would lunch there too. Surely he would not shut himself in his rooms; she would be almost certain to see him. She would know him in a moment. She wondered if he had told Cynthia about her yet. Mrs. Hennifer had not been to Old Lafer for months, she had not heard anything; had she seen her, she dare not have questioned her. She had always regretted the confidence she had given her; it was folly indeed to have thought of writing to him, to have actually begun a letter; to lose it and then to confess to it was idiotic. She wondered if that book had ever been found—the autumn rains might have reduced it to pulp long ago. But on the other hand they might not. It was possible that it had never been exposed to the rains. Some one might have found it. She had longed to ask Prissy that day if she knew anything about it but feared to do so lest she did, but had not known to whom it belonged. It had occurred to her, too, that any one finding it and the sheet of paper within might have attributed it to Miss

Marlowe. She tortured herself by trying to remember whether Cynthia knew her handwriting, she thought Anna had always written her notes to the Hall. In that case she was safe. To raise inquiry was to court suspicion and discovery——

Suddenly she started violently. One of the dogs broke the deathlike outer silence by bursting into a long howl. This raised her fears again, and increased the feeling of desperate nervousness which convinced her she might lose self-control if alone at night. She told herself again that she absolutely dare not sleep alone. This eerie sound breaking the stillness was too surely a token of death and the supernatural. She sat up, shivering miserably, and clasping her hands round her knees as she drew them up on the settee, glanced again fearfully round the room, holding her head so as to master the shadowiness of the corners into which the lamplight, shaded into concentration on the table, could not penetrate. Then she rang the bell. No one appeared. Dinah and Peggy could not hear it upstairs; and Elias, neglecting his reading aloud for once to meditate on the changes and chances of this mortal world, would not heed, as she bitterly felt, when he knew she only was in the parlour. She dare not even open the door. How was she to get to bed? No one would sympathise with her fears; no device of hers would even keep the kitchen door open while she went upstairs; what could she do?

It was then that an idea flashed with the clear keenness of lightning into her mind. There was one resource. She put her hand into her pocket. Yes, Anna *had* given her the keys, and she had them still.

CHAPTER XIX

'SIN THE GUEST'

THAT lightning flash of thought suffused her whole being with the glow of inspiration. Temptation, in the guise of escape, clutched every fibre of her innermost nature. Heat succeeded to chill, confidence to depression. Realisation of the capacities of the thought made her gasp breathless one moment; the next she succumbed.

And now her very cowardice nerved her to courage. She got up, and moving more quickly than usual crossed the room. Then she opened the door and looked into the hall.

All was quiet. Every one but Elias must still be upstairs. She could hear the monotonous creak of the rockers of his chair on the flagged floor of the kitchen, and imagined him sitting with folded hands and his head sunk on his chest, while he stared at the fire and reflected on the old times and the new, with a patriarchal sense of belonging to the old times in which he had been young. Yes, poor old Elias was nearing the threescore years and ten of the Psalmist. He might well reflect on melancholy things. But mortal corruption would not be her portion for many years. That was all she dreaded; spiritual corruption might plant its fangs deep, but so long as they implanted tardy pleasure in the starvation of her affections she would greet it. The marvellous sermon of life from the simple text 'Be good' had no import for her; the world was not a vestibule, death was not transition; for her the wilderness could only blossom as the rose by the fulfilment of earthly desire, of things of the senses, of the cravings of nature. Simple, heartfelt, disinterested goodness raised a sneer to her lips; had she spoken, it would have been to ejaculate 'Milk for babes!' in response to the plea, 'For love of Christ'; she was clever enough to feel that she condescended in attending the worship of a deity, since she did not go from mere habit; a lapse in morality was but the yielding to the lower nature, to which, as stronger than the higher, it was really more natural to yield; from looseness of conviction she had fallen to looseness of habit of thought; duty and principle held no golden rule, and now conscience was gangrenous. But all this was unexpressed. Her influence was only insidious as passive. The canker at the heart of the flower is rarely suspected until it falls in pieces and is scattered to the winds. And such a flower is not regretted. 'It was rotten,' we say. Alas! there are human souls of which we can say no otherwise; divine love alone can gather the petals and re-form the flower.

Having satisfied herself that all was quiet Mrs. Severn softly closed the parlour door again. Then she unlocked the cellarette. In one corner was a bottle of whisky, almost untouched, but nothing more either of wine or spirit. She took it up and held it to the light reflectively. It was of the nature she desired, its form did not signify. She felt no hesitation. She would take some before going upstairs, slip off her clothes, and be in bed before it took effect. Then it occurred to her that the effect might soon pass unless she fell asleep at once, and leave her the more craven because unnerved. It was certain she must have the bottle upstairs. It was, however, a problem that perplexed her as to how she was to get it there.

She could not take it now, for if Mr. Severn returned he would want it. Also, if

Dinah had put Antoinette or Emmeline into her room, she would be certain, after Emmeline's silly fright, to remain with the children until bedtime. There was, too, the fire in her room to attend to. She did not fear Peggy, but Dinah had lynx eyes and sense. She tried to think of every possibility, and found it an absorbing interest. She was now determined to brave the definite from fear of the indefinite. It was a risk to take the bottle out of the cellarette and put it in the secretaire, but that was necessary, for Dinah might demand the keys at any moment for some household want. If Mr. Severn came she would hear him in time to put it back in the sideboard if she still had the keys, or to place it on the table for use. Then, again, she thought it safer against suspicion to place it on the sideboard now, conspicuously, as a matter of course, that it might be considered ready for Mr. Severn. She further took the trouble to open the second closet of the sideboard and find a sugar-basin and glasses. After this she returned to the sofa and lay down, and impressed her programme for all contingencies on her mind. She now felt fortified and exhilarated. A sleepless night was not before her. After all, what more reasonable than to drug terrors that would not be exorcised, being, as they were, the result of an extreme sensibility that might eventually induce nervous disease? Surely it was intended that the anæsthetic qualities of alcohol should thus be utilised.

Presently Peggy brought in supper. In answer to Mrs. Severn's questions she said that Dinah had taken the iron bed-chair into Miss Emmeline's room, and Miss Antoinette was to sleep with her, and Dinah would not leave them. No one was in Mrs. Severn's room. Peggy, having heard all that Dinah had been told by the children, delivered this defiantly, and was surprised at the calmness with which it was taken. Mrs. Severn was relieved. She would rather not have one of the girls with her now. She would sleep this sleep alone. In one thing she must trust to Providence—that she would not be roused to admit her husband.

Ten o'clock struck.

But now that the time had come she felt again how great was the risk, so great that nothing short of desperation could authorise her to run into it. She knew her husband's unbounded kindness of heart. No matter how heavy the pressure of business, she would be on his mind. He would make every effort to get home that night. He would think of her not only as dull but as 'timid.' She was certain still that he would come if he could, and that if he could not it would be the storm that would prevent him; nothing less than impassable roads would daunt him. Had any further emergency obliged him to stay the night at Lafer Hall, he would have let her know.

She went again to the window, and cautiously throwing up the sash leant out. It was snowing heavily, and there was a depth of some inches on the sill; the world was white and muffled, she could scarcely penetrate as far as the garden wall through the eddying whirl of flakes. From this she could judge how stormy it would be in the lanes that her husband would have to traverse between the Hall and East Lafer. But no fear for his safety disturbed her. It never occurred to her that he might even then be struggling against the storm on a spent horse. She had not thought of placing a light in a window, hoping it might guide him. Anna would have done that. She never did. She only stood and listened intently, so alive to the situation that had she heard a shout of distress it would not have surprised her; but unstirred by any emotion, wishing only to satisfy herself that there was no fear of his coming now, that the roads must be impracticable for night-travelling.

At last, chilled through, she closed the window again and re-arranged the curtains. Reason pointed to safety for herself. Yet a presentiment of evil weighed upon her. She stood against the table, indecision in her attitude and expression, but with feverish eyes fixed upon the sideboard. It was not now fear of the supernatural, but craving for alcohol, that overwhelmed her. She knew that if she took that bottle upstairs she would drink, and if she left it down she would saturate sugar with eau-de-cologne and take that. It was no longer that she could not brave her fancies, the terrors of the flickering firelight, of darkness, the crackling of the wood in the grate, the creaking of boards, the sobbing of the wind behind the wainscot, the rushing of rats overhead in the unused attics, the ticking of the clock on the landing that now sounded distant, then near, as though an invisible hand had opened her door. She shuddered as she thought of them, but she was self-deceived. The courage she had gained during her preoccupation did not ebb; but it was mastered by the fact that self-indulgence of a rare kind was at her command.

A shawl that she wore in winter when moving about the cold stone passages was flung over the back of the sofa. She went and mechanically took it up. Throwing it over her shoulders, she then hid the bottle within it lest she should meet Dinah or Peggy upstairs.

And now she was filled with reckless courage. The old awful thirst was upon her. She woke into life and eagerness; her lips moved involuntarily, producing a sensation in her throat as though she were already swallowing the craved-for draught; her eyes dilated and gleamed with greedy anticipation of the fumes that were soon to confuse her brain. She trembled violently as the thought flashed across her that never before had she had such an opportunity for enjoyment. Excitement worked in her and affected her feverishly.

She lit her bedroom candle, intending to extinguish the lamp at once. But instead of doing so she took up a tumbler. Then, without a moment's hesitation, she opened the shawl and uncorking the bottle poured out some of the spirit. She drank it raw, sip by sip.

And now she must get upstairs at once. Already she felt a delicious tingling of warmth in her veins. In a few minutes she might find herself unable to walk steadily. In her haste she confused lamp and candle, blew out the latter and barely escaped overturning the lamp by the fringe of her shawl catching the regulator. She relit the candle at the fire—how heavy her head was, her eyes were dancing, she could not see clearly!

She again attempted to turn out the lamp. Where was the regulator? Now her fingers were on it. But she turned it the wrong way, and the flame flared above the chimney. More by instinct than sense she reversed it. Her trembling uncertain fingers grasped the candlestick—she was ready.

It was at that very moment that the outside silence was again broken by what seemed to her confused senses a confusion of sounds; a shout, faint first but instantly repeated loudly, barks and yelps from the dogs, a sudden stir of chairs, doors, and voices in the kitchen. In the supreme terror of the situation she almost fell, but saved herself by clutching the table. She struggled to listen. Could this be her husband? Forcing back the tingling fire from her clouded brain she did listen. She heard the gate clash and voices coming nearer.

Frenzy seized her. She had no power left to think; her limbs well-nigh refused to support her. But she knew she must reach her room, hide herself—— She forgot what she would leave upon the table. She did not know she had overturned the bottle. Seizing the candlestick again she stumbled to the door. With a wrench she flung it open, nearly losing her balance, for she was unprepared for it opening upon herself and had tried to push it. She gained the stairs, reeling against the banisters, then recovering herself. At the last turn the candlestick fell from her hands and rolled down from step to step. But by dint of the door of her room being open and showing the firelight, she reached her room and sank upon the settee.

Mr. Severn came into the hall, wiping his beard from the snow that had melted in it. He had taken off his topcoat and gaiters in the kitchen with Dinah's help. They had talked of the Admiral and Mrs. Marlowe, and he had omitted to ask if his wife were still up. In fact he rarely asked particulars about her either of Elias or Dinah; their strong prejudice showed itself in their resentful indifference, and this he made a point of overlooking. Neither was Dinah anxious to be questioned. She could not trouble him, weary and worn-out as he was, with an account of the evening's catastrophe and only that would have excused her in his opinion for not having been in the parlour.

He went on to the parlour. The door was open, Clothilde then was gone to bed. The moment he was within the door he smelt the strong smell of spirits. There was still a good fire in the grate, but its flicker did not illumine the table. He had stood still, transfixed with amazement at that smell and an extraordinary impression of confusion which he gleaned even in the dusk. Now, he started forward and dashed the poker among the turves. They leapt into a blaze. He turned and looked at the table. Its confusion was indeed horrible. The cloth was pulled awry and soaked by the spirit still dribbling from the overturned bottle; the empty glass, the blackened chimney of the lamp, all told their tale. His face blanched. He clenched his hand over the mantelpiece edge to steady himself. In an instant he was overwhelmed with raging emotions of despair, amazement, horror, a desperate foreboding. Whose work was this? Where was Clothilde?

He tried to shout for Dinah but the words died in his throat, producing a dry rattle. He rushed back to the door and met her there, carrying a tray. He clutched her arm.

'Dinah,' he said, 'who—what—Almighty God, where is my wife?'

Dinah had but to look round the door and she knew all.

MRS. SEVERN

PART II

CHAPTER I

SPRINGTIME

DANBY and Cynthia were walking on the terrace at Lafer. Danby was again staying at the 'Marlowe Arms' in Wonston and had come to the Hall early in the day.

It was the first English spring he had had for many years and he enjoyed it. The freshness of the sunny air made him restless—at least so he said, but as this wore off when he each day reached Lafer, Cynthia was dubious. From his bedroom window he looked over to the moors that lay softly blue against the vapoury sky. The Lafer woods were bursting into leaf; there was a flush on the larches betwixt Old Lafer and the pits; the shadow mouldings were softened by a haze of golden sunshine.

Danby had gathered some primroses and given them to Cynthia. They gleamed in the crape of her dress.

'I was almost inclined to commit the atrocity of a walk before breakfast this morning,' he said.

'Well, why didn't you? That's the time to see the butterflies asleep on the flowers.'

'I fear I should not have seen either.'

'But they choose the largest flowers, they are very fond of the ox-eye daisy. So am I, but I really prefer the little ones of spring, violets that scent the air but hide themselves, and snowdrops peeping from the moss of the woods and scarcely venturing to look at one.'

'Oh, Cynthia, a pretty conceit! I aver that they fear the winds of adversity and prefer caution to cold.'

'You may aver what you please. It will be something practical of course.'

'Why *of course*? Come, you nineteenth century women are bound to be logical. It's evolution, you cannot escape the obligation. I shall insult your chivalry of sex if I ask is it because of mine?'

'How can it be, Lucius? Think of our poets. No, it is yourself. Are you ever anything but practical?'

'Yes, in Zante and St. Helier's. I was self-convicted when Kerr exploded his bomb and I found myself a dreaming fool.'

Cynthia laughed, but her hand trembled as she touched the flowers in her waistband.

'Do you know what Theo told me? she said.

'Something Kerr told her, I suppose.'

'He said for one moment you looked as though you would throw me over.'

'What more reasonable when I found how I had been taken in?'

'You should have been more practical,' she said.

They both laughed, Cynthia looking up at him to enjoy the brightening of his face. It constantly brightened now. She had once told him she thought it was her mission in life to make him look happy.

It was deliciously warm on the terrace. They had meant to go farther. They generally did, but forgot. The woods were lovely, but the path was narrow; the park was beautiful, especially where the lake reflected the chestnuts sweeping its margin, but there was a feeling of uneasiness on Cynthia's part as regarded the cattle; in the road they met people whom Cynthia could not pass without a word; the moors, tempting in the distance, were too rough for easy conversation. But the terrace was bathed in sunshine, and their eyes loved to wander over the view. The wallflowers under the windows loaded the air with warm perfume.

Betwixt the cedars were gleams of the tulips edging the bowling-green. And the birds were singing all round, adding love as a charm to life.

Cynthia had never known them sing so sweetly. She told herself it was in contrast to the long storm and her sorrows. Mrs. Marlowe's frail life had flickered out soon after the Admiral's death. For the last few months Cynthia's time had been chiefly given to business. She insisted on being initiated in all its mysteries, and gaining practical knowledge for the management of her estates. Tremenheere imparted complicated details to her while mastering them himself. She saw much more of him than of Danby. Danby indeed, when he came down from town, felt himself in the way. Tremenheere was constantly at the Hall, closeted in the library with Mr. Severn or the lawyers, and Cynthia's presence with them was often indispensable. He was reduced to solitary strolls or to talks with Mrs. Hennifer.

His position had not been one of the pleasantest. Sweet and confiding as Cynthia was to him, it made him jealous to see Tremenheere's well-established footing, and to hear her appeal to him for advice. On the other hand, he felt that the lawyers and Mr. Severn were not more than civilly tolerating. The conditions of the will were irritating. Nothing had been altered after his engagement to Cynthia; there were clauses that brought conspicuously forward the Admiral's time-worn affection for Anthony Tremenheere, and suggested the conviction that he would always be the nearest in her reliance. They were all prejudiced, considering him an interloper and mistrusting him as an alien of ungauged character. They were saturated with traditional veneration for the Marlowes and personal affection for Cynthia. They had intended her to marry Tremenheere. Probably had she not now been engaged to himself she would have become engaged to the Canon at this crisis. In thinking of them he recalled a certain essay of Bacon's. Tremenheere was of that 'grave nature, led by custom and therefore constant'; Cynthia of that 'chastity which is often proud,' though in her case too unconscious to presume upon any merit.

But now he was having her more to himself. The press of business was over, and routine work, requiring an hour or two a day, was arranged so as not to interfere with him. It was evident she wished to be with him and to draw him into her life.

She had come out to-day, determined to talk. Since he told her of his old attachment to Mrs. Severn she had not named the subject. Not that it had been on her mind. After the first shock of surprise at the incongruity of the fact, she reduced her pride by rapid reasoning on the side of common sense, and turned to him with greater frankness than she had ever shown. But it occurred to her afterwards, and Mrs. Hennifer urged upon her, that there should be perfect unreserve on the point. Yet she scarcely knew what to say. It is difficult to revert to a matter of vital importance that has once been dismissed as concluded.

They had left the terrace and strolled across the bowling-green into a plantation of silver birches. A winding path led through it to a gate into the park. The trees were not thickly planted, here too the Admiral and his woodman had hewn down and lopped. Each slender stem rose pillar-like and isolated. The sun, filtering through the tracery of fresh foliage, silvered the new bark or dappled the moss and primroses with golden glints. There was a faint rustling of leaves, like tiny birds trying their wings, Cynthia thought. They leant against the gate.

From here the park trended upwards, due north to the moors. Danby traced a track through the grass.

'The hares have known where to come for food this winter,' he said, pointing to it.

'I don't think the hares have anything to do with this,' said Cynthia. 'See how straight it runs to the woods. There's a stile where it ends. The woods skirt the moors and there are no hares there. I have seen grouse come down here. It is a path to the pits and the Mires, just as this lower one'—she turned and pointed in another direction—'goes to another stile that leads through into the Old Lafer woods. Some day we'll go to the Mires, Lucius, and you shall see the forlornest little place you ever imagined, a tumbledown hamlet in a hollow with a marsh.'

'And do you mean to tolerate tumble-down hamlets, Miss Marlowe?'

'This isn't worth keeping up—a nest of poachers, grandpapa used to call it. I really want to go and see it for myself; for I have an idea about it, such a utilitarian one that I feel I shall establish my reputation as a business woman with Anthony and Mr. Severn. But I won't tell it until I am sure it is feasible.'

'And do you think yourself capable of judging alone of its feasibility?' asked Danby with a smile.

'Quite. I can judge of your tone too. It means "*What a poor little idea this must be that's all her own!*"'

'I did not know you had such insight!' said he.

'If I were you I would not confess to such ignorance,' she retorted, in the gayest of spirits. But still she was conscious of the rift within the lute and her own shrinking.

There was silence. The air was so delicious that Danby took off his hat the better to enjoy it. Cynthia was gazing at the sky that was full of vapoury lights and drifts of sultry gray, slowly sailing above the wood-crowned hill.

'Lucius,' she said at last, with an involuntary little sigh, 'have you ever seen Mrs. Severn yet?'

He turned quickly and looked at her.

'I believe I have,' he said.

'Really?' she said, her face flushing with surprise rather than with relief at the indifference of his tone.

'Must I describe the apparition and then you can make me certain about its identity?' he said.

'Yes. Let us walk back.'

'No. Let us stay here,' he said, with an instant's slipping of his arm around her waist. 'Come, my darling Cynthy, you shall not even feel this as derogatory to your dignity of social position. You said so little, you were so sweet when first I told you, that I have felt since I should insult you by attributing wounded pride to you;' and as she yielded to his wish, and propping her elbows on the gate, laid her cheek on her hands and looked at him, he went on, 'I have always meant to tell you that the Hugos are of as good birth as yourself, though far from being heiresses. And you have been in Jersey, and went out to St. Brelade's to see the Pitons. You know they are of the aristocracy of the islands. Miss Hugo married much beneath her. I had not any idea whom she married or where she was until that day when—within a few hours—Piton and Kerr told me where she was and who you were. Kerr had no clue to the shock he gave me. But my mind soon adjusted itself to all the facts and their grouping. I was only anxious for your sake. I saw at once that to many women this trick of fate might be a great mortification.'

'But I showed you that it was not to me,' said Cynthia slowly. 'That is what Mrs. Hennifer too feels. It is inexplicable.'

'To you it is,' said Danby, his face lighting up with that smile that smoothed its furrows and renewed its youth. 'You are far removed by nature from envy and jealousy; it is nature, not circumstance, that guides one away from the debasing side of this life's vicissitudes. Thank Heaven you are what you are! Don't you know, Cynthia, what this ingenuous affection of yours is to me, after what I have gone through; how it reverses my cynicism, and makes a woman after all into what she should be to us men, a guardian angel, a guiding star? I little thought a year ago—just before I met you—that a woman would ever have the influence over me that you have. And you, who might have married better men both in——'

But she interrupted him, half laughing, half crying.

'Don't, Lucius!'

'Well, you are not self-seeking but wholly womanly, divinely womanly,' he said with ardent devotion in voice and look. She had never thought he would make so devoted a lover, had never dreamt she should be wooed as he wooed her! And he had never dreamt he could woo as he did! It was the goodness in each nature that struck fire by friction.

'Ah! if more women were like you there would be many better men in the world,' he exclaimed involuntarily, and before she knew he had turned to her and folded her in his arms.

'Oh, Cynthia!' he said, releasing her again with a sense of adoration of her flushed face, and the shy sweet eyes that met his with a daunted air of surprised subjugation. 'You little guess what demons possess some women!' He laughed satirically. 'I have seen it even on Indian stations where men swarm. And I shall never forget the quarrelling that went on on one of my passages from Port Said to Bombay in one of the ladies' cabins. They fought over space for their gowns, and their arguments were logical indeed, based on every rung in the social ladder. One stamped her foot and screamed, "Do you know I am a Colonel's daughter?" The other positively shouted, "And do you know I am a Colonel's *wife?*" Pitiful, wasn't it? Mere extraneous circumstance usurping the place of virtue and soul's worth—of Christianity, in fact! Not that I thought much then of woman's Christianity, it was scarcely invading even the Zenanas. But it did strike me they might have been more decent, showed some sense of an Eternity in which there will not be Colonelcies. Heaven preserve you from such debasement!

'And now you shall tell me if I have seen Clothilde Severn,' he said after an instant's pause, in which she heard him sigh deeply, and was conscious also that he looked at her with an affection that was almost impatient in its intensity. She was silent, overawed by the strong rush of his heart's life to hers. It seemed that this cold calm man held in check a volcano of passionate aspiration for her, and thence for himself. Oh that she might never fail him and renew the old grip of iron in his soul!

It was one day on a previous visit that Danby had seen Mrs. Severn. He was going up to Lafer to dine; the carriage had to call for him on its return from the station with Cynthia, who had been on business to a firm of solicitors in Leeds with Mr. Severn. Scarcely knowing how to pass his time, he sauntered down to the Minster. The bell was ringing for afternoon prayers, and the choir men and boys were entering the west porch. He went round to that on the north. Just as he reached the top step the inner crimson door was pulled open and a child's voice exclaimed,

'Mother, tell Joan not to push me. I shall fall down the steps.'

'You are the bigger, Emmeline, surely you can push her,' said a low, slow voice.

'There, Joan, now you mustn't or I will.'

'I'll cry if you do, Em.'

'Well, it'll be your fault, won't it, mother?'

'You must not make Joan cry, or we shall have to leave her; put you back into the Minster alone, Joan.'

Danby, at the first sound of voices, had retreated. There was not space in the porch for himself and a family group, and they were all too much absorbed in each other to see him. He had caught a glimpse of them as the door opened, and been sufficiently astonished to wish to see more. It seemed such a handsome group, a modern Reynolds! Mrs. Severn came forward with her eyes down. A boy and girl had hold of either hand. Her long skirts were gathered over one arm; her bonnet of black lace, with its strings tied in a negligent bow, gave her face the soft creamy moulding of ivory. There were four children, their accent was charming, if not their temper. Their style was gipsy-like, black serge frocks with crimson scarves, and large hats with crimson ribbons, set off their dusky skin, long dark hair and lustrous eyes. He thought they belonged to the Close, perhaps were the family of the Canon in Residence. They jumped from step to step, and their mother slowly followed. He was standing motionless in the shadow of a buttress and she did not see him. The children did, stared vivaciously, but said nothing. His glance wandered from one to another, and rested with a sudden startled inquiry of recognition upon Mrs. Severn. Had she looked up he must have known her and she him.

But she did not. He allowed her to pass,

relieved at the moment that she did. But later, having analysed his sensations and realised that he had been affected by nothing more than surprise and curiosity, he would have been glad had they bowed to each other. A remark of Mrs. Hennifer's rankled in his mind, and sometimes teased him with misgiving as to Mrs. Severn's presuming upon reminiscence. He was certain that in spite of what her eyes fixed upon him might have betrayed, he could have daunted her then, once for all.

The whole of this he now told Cynthia. It was not necessary that she should assure him his conjecture was right, her glance as he described the group was sufficient.

There was a moment's silence when his voice ceased. He looked down at her, watching a faint shade that stole over her face.

'What is the trouble, Cynthy?' he said.

She smiled, and drawing nearer laid her

cheek against his arm, half caressingly, half shamefacedly.

'Oh! I am very silly,' she said; 'but I wish you had spoken and been done with it. I wish she had seen you, Lucius.'

'Darling, whom do you mistrust?' he asked, bending to catch the answer that he knew could only be a whisper.

'Oh, Lucius!' she murmured.

'Well then, since it is not me, why and what do you fear?'

She looked up at him, a world of love in her guileless eyes.

'Nothing,' she said aloud. To her own heart she added, 'Except perhaps myself.'

'Keep to that,' he said. 'Never suffer yourself to pursue phantoms, Cynthy.'

What wonder, when she looked so artlessly ashamed, that he should kiss her again!

'To give you courage, my sweet one,' he whispered, as his lips withdrew themselves, and he saw peace shine again in her eyes.

CHAPTER II

AN ENCOUNTER ON THE MOOR

Cynthia did not forget her intention of going to the Mires. She proposed too that they should walk.

'You shall get an idea of what walking through ling is,' she said. 'You say you have never been on a moor, but you must be before you attempt to shoot one. The keepers will disdain you if you can't clear the fibre and steady your aim in plunging through a hummock. They know nothing of jungle work, and will think any child might shoot such a big thing as a tiger. But grouse, that come with a rush like a tempest and elude you even when they are in packs that darken the air, are the "tickliest fowl" that can befool a gun.'

'Still, if you fire wildly and miss, you are not in the same predicament as when you miss a tiger, to whom it is simply a friendly invitation to come on,' said Danby.

'You speak with feeling,' Cynthia said.

'I have been between a tiger's claws,' said Danby. 'But happily for me they were sheathed at the moment.'

It was a gloriously bright crisp day when they went to the Mires. The sun shone, brightening the bilberry beds into vividest green and red amid the still rusty ling. In the hollows patches of silver-green spagnum nestled round pools or clumps of velvet rush marked a watercourse. Sun-rays streamed in vistas on the horizon, pearling the haze on the distant hills. The sailing cloud shadows eclipsed the sunshine, now here, then there, in endless change. It was impossible not to stop at every few steps and feast on the colour that sun and air wooed from old Earth.

'I always imagined a moor to be dreary and solemn,' said Danby once when they were standing thus. All was so beautiful that the rapt look of delight on Cynthia's face was as it were its index.

'Like Egdon Heath in the first chapter,' said Cynthia. 'When you are on them just after the sun has sunk they are; yes, most solemn in their air of eternal changelessness. Alderdale Tarn and Black Dyke are always so. But on days like this I am always convinced they love their own beautiful steadfastness, and feel a nearness to Heaven. Oh! I hope they will never be swept and garnished for the seven devils of our surplus population! I dread the political economist of the future who may set the mobs to level and drain, and pare and scrape Olympus!'

Danby laughed.

'Well said, Cynthia,' he exclaimed. 'Olympus with reservoirs is bad enough. One might die of Olympus with streets and railroads, telephone switch-boards and pneumatic tubes for letters. I declare these heathery hills should make recluses; their prodigality of colour is too luxurious for mere anchorites, but transcendentalists now who want a surfeit of sky might bring their mittens here. It's far more healthy than Thoreau's woods round Walden Pool.'

In fact, at their rate of progress to-day, it took them two hours to reach the Mires.

They did not descend into the hollow. Danby wanted Cynthia to go to one of the cottages and rest. He noticed Hartas Kendrew's at once as more decent than the others; the pots of geranium and checked curtains proved it. But Cynthia suspected this was Kendrew's and would have gone there less readily than to another. She leant upon her alpenstock and rested, while glancing thoughtfully from the glistening scaly-like marsh to the ruined cottages that seemed to mock the others rather than to be mocked by them. Danby watched her silent calculation with amusement.

'I hope you are not going to set an example to the economists,' he said.

'I believe I am,' she said. 'I'll tell you what I think, Lucius. You know I mean to rebuild that narrow old peaked bridge between Wonston and Lafer. We shall want stone. Here is good stone, ready hewn. Why should we not use it, and do away with its reproach to us here?'

'Capital! unless there's any chance of more coal seams and pit-men.'

'I don't think there is. The seams are all poor. Three or four men and one horse work them; even since I remember they have been worked out and new shafts sunk. Sometimes the men go down, sometimes into the ground, laterally. We'll go back that way, and you shall see what poor stuff they get for their labour.'

'Fit for your greenhouses, I suppose. But, Cynthia, you will tire yourself if the pits take us farther.'

'Only round,' she said. 'There's a short cut through the Old Lafer plantations that will bring us at right angles to the park-track. Besides, I feel as though I could walk for ever in this air.'

'I don't know whether it makes my heels feel most like a deer or a gutta-percha ball,' said Danby. 'It tempers the vagaries of the ling fibre. I shall not disgrace you before the keepers—is this one coming along?'

They had struck the coal-road, and as he spoke there appeared on the ridge of a slope they were mounting a short thick-set figure in corduroys, and a mongrel dog running in and out of the ling with its nose to the ground. The moment the man saw them he called the cur to heel, just strangling its yelp of delight as it raised a grouse. The bird rose with a whirr and flying low and heavily dropped almost immediately on to a rock and bragged at them. The man and dog advanced slouchingly, an evil-looking pair. It was Hartas. His eyes were fastened on Danby. He had recognised Cynthia, but Danby he had not seen before.

'It is not a keeper, it's one of the pit-men,' said Cynthia. 'We won't stop, he's a bad old man, a poacher they say, and a drunkard. Just nod to him, Lucius. How he stares at you!'

But Hartas had made up his mind to stop.

'Good-day, Mistress,' he said touching his hat. 'It's a terrible fine day, but I didn't ken you were so rare and bigoted o' t' Mires as to foul your feet wi' our slime. And I hope t' quality called in passing.'

'We did not go down. Miss Marlowe is

thinking of making some improvements that will tidy you up a bit,' said Danby.

'And how is your daughter? It was her whom I saw the day of the Northside Edge sale, was it not?' said Cynthia pleasantly.

'Ay, Priscilla's my daughter, leastways inasmuch as she's my son's wife. I mind that sale too, a bad job it wer for us, cost us the best old nag ever I harnessed into shafts, thanks to a party as wer riding a high-stepper hersel, and maybe had more on 'em in her stables——'

'But you got another directly,' Cynthia burst in eagerly, her face flushing at the injustice rather than the insolence. 'I inquired; Canon Tremenheere inquired for me, and he happened to come across the very man from whom you bought it. It was bought and paid for, or I should have sent your daughter some money.'

'And couldn't you mind how it straightened us?' said Hartas with a wheedling drop of his voice. 'If you'd gone down to-day and opened wer door you'd hev seen as fine a young fellow as ever stepped straightened on wer settle, and Doctor Borlase ordering wine and jelly, and Scilla breaking her heart to get 'em. But nay, nay, the likes o' you wi' t' long purses pass us by, and when we gang to t' rabbit-burrows that nobbut breed what you reckon vermin, you come down sharp and clap us into gaol to waste wer lives out.'

Danby would have interrupted this impudence, but Cynthia made a forbidding gesture. Nor would she walk on, as he suggested in an undertone. She faced Hartas with her figure drawn up, and a blaze of indignation in her eyes.

'Grouse are not vermin,' she said. 'And your son not only poached grouse but, by his own confession, committed manslaughter. Do you mean that he's home from prison?'

'Ay, I do. On ticket o' leave. Ticket o' death, I call it.'

'He is ill, then?'

'He is that! Them that kenned him afore as that lingy and thewy he'd bear a tempest's blast like a willow-tree and show no rent, don't ken him now. He's a curiosity-like for all t' neighbours, that skeletonish, wi' his ribs showing like a starved dog.'

'I'm very sorry. I'll see Mr. Borlase,' said Cynthia.

'*Sorry's* a thin word for them as made the sorrow. And you and t' Admiral you're all one, t' same flesh and blood. Two grudges I bear you and that's on my oath,' said Hartas, his face purpling until the veins stood out like whip-cord.

'And I lay you're the chap she'll wed, Mr. Lucius Danby, eh?' he added, suddenly controlling himself. He turned and stared again at Danby with a glower that changed into a leer.

Danby expected some vile oath would drop from him.

'Cynthia, we've had sufficient of this,' he said, putting his hand on her arm.

But she hesitated another moment, too stunned by the brutal allusion to her grandfather to realise that she was expected to obey. In that moment Hartas let fly his last gibe.

'And are you taking him back by Old Lafer to see Mistress Severn?' he said, chuckling. 'Ay, I ken what's sent her to drink and damnation! Would ta like to see what I found, t' bit o'——'

He was fumbling in his breast pocket and looking from one to the other with gloating triumph. It was a shot at random after all. But it went home with sickening horror to Cynthia's heart and inspired Danby with a brute's fell rage. He sprang at him and bore him to the ground and left him there with a kick. Then he took Cynthia's arm and made her lean upon him, pressing and caressing both her hands. But for a little while he did not dare to look at her.

There were hard sobs, knotty and stifling, in Cynthia's throat. She did not cry. Not a tear sprang to her eyes as yet, but she had turned white and he felt her tremble. When at last their eyes met there was piteous entreaty in hers, a wounded surprise that welled from the bottom of her heart.

'It was so cruel,' she gasped.

'It was more, it was vile,' said Danby with deep rage in his voice. 'Such a thing was inconceivable! The fellow was in liquor. If you knew what he was you should not have argued with him; such crooked minds never see reason or right. I could not have imagined it possible you would be so insulted. And how could he make such an insinuation? Can there be any truth in it, in the degradation—*her* degradation, I mean? What was he going to show us?'

'Was he going to show us anything? Wasn't it deception? What could he have to show us to implicate her?'

'And yet how could he have got the clue?'

'To associate you with her; how indeed?'

'How in the name of Heaven does this old reprobate know what he assumes? Does every one know? What has he to do with the Severns? I think no woman in possession of her sober senses would associate her name with mine under the circumstances.'

'Oh! I don't know,' said Cynthia wearily.

She looked round with a sudden feeling of forlorn incomprehension. Had the sun gone in? No, it still shone. She chided herself for her misery. Was not Danby at her side? Had he not proved his chivalrous love for her? Was not his grief the deeper for hers? She made an effort to throw off her depression, to smile again.

But a little complaint escaped her involuntarily.

'Oh I wish, I wish that things were not as they are,' she said, sighing.

'What can we do?' said Danby.

'They might go, you know; the Severns—leave Old Lafer, I mean. But how could I send them away, he such a trusty old servant and friend of grandpapa's, and so good to me! Then Anna is going to marry so happily into Wonston! And how could I do it? What could I say? I don't think he can know. But it is her, Mrs. Severn. And yet I never see her unless I go specially to Old Lafer, she so rarely leaves home. I cannot understand it. Mrs. Hennifer assured me Anna did not know of you, still less any one else. What dreadful things he said!'

'The most dreadful, *drink and damnation.*'

'Can there be any truth in it?'

'None, I should say.'

'I have never heard of her drinking,

Lucius. But we might be the last to hear. She is odd. She has left home sometimes and gone to the Mires.'

'To the Mires! What an unearthly hole to choose! For a day, do you mean?'

'No, for weeks.'

'Cynthia! With whom could she stay there?'

The same thought flashed into each mind. They stopped and looked at each other.

'Was it at Kendrew's?' said Danby.

'Yes, it was. His daughter-in-law used to be nursemaid to her children.'

'Then he may have spoken the truth,' said Danby quietly. 'He *may* know.'

CHAPTER III

CYNTHIA FACES THE SITUATION

THE shock of this encounter with Kendrew was much greater to Danby than to Cynthia. Her buoyancy of spirit made the recoil from sorrow rapid although its impression was ineffaceable. But he was not of buoyant temperament. He realised too, better than she could, the hidden danger. Again and again his thoughts recurred to Kendrew's boast of possessing a proof. Why had he been so hasty? He should have demanded it and then knocked him down. His blood boiled at the insult offered to Cynthia. Then again he shuddered at the reflection of what

Mrs. Severn might do were she indeed irresponsible. He thought of going to the Mires and insisting upon Kendrew proving the truth of his words and relinquishing his proof if it were indeed in tangible form on paper. But little would be gained by this. He knew Cynthia would never consent to buy his silence. The mere fact of his having been in early youth engaged to Mrs. Severn dwindled before that of her being a degraded woman in close proximity to them.

And who knew the truth? Did Severn, after all; or Borlase or Tremenheere or even Mrs. Hennifer? Did Miss Hugo? He had not met Miss Hugo yet; he had constantly missed her when at the Hall. He had never again seen Mrs. Severn. He wished to do so now in order to make closer observations. His whole being was steeled against her with a deadly repugnance. One thing was certain, Cynthia must consent to hasten their marriage. She wished to defer it for a year.

But he was determined she should give him the full right to guard her from insult, and to track evil to its lair.

'Come, my darling, you must consent to take me at once,' he said one day when they had again talked all over and she was looking wearied with fruitless speculations. 'We both want a quiet wedding. Why put it off until your friends and the county will expect a gay one. Go up to town with me and get Mrs. Kerr to shop with you and let us drive off from St. Peter's to Victoria one morning. A thorough change will do you good, and we'll stay away as long as you like.'

'I shall not want to stay away long,' she said. 'Perhaps you will. Are you sure you won't find Lafer dull?'

They were in the library. Cynthia sauntered to the window and leant against one of the mullions. Danby, sitting at the writing-table, looked up and watched her. Her figure was outlined by the soft sunshine that streamed along the terrace, without as yet reaching more than the curve of her cheek and glistening on her golden hair. But how lovely she was! The black dress, fitting exquisitely yet falling in soft and ample folds to the ground, set off her dazzling fairness and subtly toned the vivacity and buoyancy of her gestures. She was in the responsive mood he loved.

'I shall never find our life here together dull,' he said, going and standing beside her. 'Cynthia,' he went on half-playfully, 'there is only one thing you must try to do, even I have not succeeded in teaching it to you, and that is you must try to think more of yourself relatively; of your own value, I mean. You never really seem to wish to impress me, or to wonder if you please me. Yet I am sure it is not because you don't care, or because you take it as a matter of course. You are not independent, and yet you have not misgivings as the dependent often have. But simply you don't think of yourself. You just act from a sense of right, and glean your happiness in the result——'

'No, no, what nonsense!' she said. 'You are wrong. I didn't become engaged to you from a sense of right, Lucius.'

'Well, we will except that. Exceptions are required to prove the rule, you know. But apart from that you never say, "Do you like me in this," or "Am I doing as you wish," or "I should like it so and so." I don't mean that I ask you to consult with me, only to feel that whatever you do or wish is of paramount importance to me, would in fact be my guide and moral barometer. Advise with whom you like. You have old and tried heads at command, but remember that no one can be more interested in you than myself, and that incidents become events in the close bond of married life, whether they affect one or the other, or are mutual.'

'But I am sure that by the time we get home again I shall want to consult you in everything,' she said. 'I have often been afraid of bothering you or I should now. Then you see Anthony not only knows but remembers. Grandpapa and he used to walk and talk or ride together over the estate, so he has all at his finger ends. But it is not only that I like to say to him, "Do you remember?"'

'I covet Tremenheere's reminiscences!' said Danby. 'He would know you as a golden-curled child, as a slender slip of a girl, as a sunbeam in society. I come in as an afterthought of Nature's.'

'Then Nature and I are not in sympathy. Far from it! The "perfect whole" can never be an afterthought. Don't idealise me, Lucius. I always felt that Anthony Tremenheere did in spite of old acquaintance. It will depress and cramp me if I think you idealise me. I shall be certain that some day I shall fail you in some way. Think me clay now, before you marry me. Do you know those lines of Emerson's :—

> " The lover watched his graceful maid
>   As 'mid the virgin train she strayed,
>   Nor knew her beauty's best attire
>   Was woven still by the snow-white quire ;
>   At last she came to his hermitage,
>   Like the bird from the woodlands to the cage,—
>   The gay enchantment was undone,
>   A gentle wife, but fairy none." '

'And what more do I ask for than *a gentle wife ?*' he said, as her voice dropped, faltering with shy earnestness. 'I don't want a year off your age, or more ethereal proportions, or wings sprouting from your shoulders. I think Emerson a better hand at prose than poetry, except when he lands you in poetical prose before you know where you are. I don't idealise you.'

'I'm only afraid you think me good,' she said. 'At any rate you do make me think of myself whatever you may say; and when you say " You are quite right, Cynthia," and look so proud and pleased, I think "What should I do if ever he were angry or disappointed?"'

'What is the use of harassing yourself over such remote contingencies?' he said, with caressing indulgence of amusement.

'Still it is possible?'

'Everything is possible.'

'But this is not improbable.'

'Casuist!'

'Seriously, Lucius, do you think it likely you never will be vexed with me?'

'No. But I do think I shall never be vexed by you.'

'Now you are splitting straws, and I never can. My mind is too large and yet not sufficiently elastic.'

'Who is splitting straws now? But seriously, Cynthia, I don't expect that either you or I shall not make mistakes or suffer from differences of opinion. But what are they but the rivets to the bolt? Who but a fool would disparage an opinion because it was not his own?'

'We are not all so wise as to see the value of dissent,' said Cynthia. 'And I, being only a woman, might lose my temper, or forget my principles, or stifle my judgment, and yet resent a rebuke.'

'I will never rebuke you,' said Danby.

'Then you would break my heart!' she cried vehemently.

'No, no, your conscience would adjust all before it was too late.'

'But you speak as though I were better than you.'

'I thought you were. I am not one who believes that "woman is the lesser man"; far from that! I believe she is the leading moral power. How many women there are of whom it might be said, if only people would think, what has been said of Beatrice in Florence, "The city was the better for her presence." And if the city, surely the home.'

'I shall begin to be sure I shall not satisfy you.'

'A little self-distrust won't do any harm,' he said, laughing. 'Still, don't try. There are some persons one can't bear to see *trying*. Nature has given them gifts of instinct and perception that make effort a hoax, and one feel as though they were caricaturing themselves. To do and to dare are equally simple and natural; they haven't to pause and consider what's right. The right thought only is in their hearts.'

'But, Lucius, believe at least that I shall probably do wrong now and then. Do unsaint me!'

'I do. But really I have not sainted you.'

'I don't believe my judgment might fail so much as my heart,' she said wistfully, after a little pause.

'Oh, Cynthia, I should always know the

pure motive was there, yes, and the good intention and strong principle.'

'Would you forgive me?'

'When you were my wife, dearest?'

His tone of tenderest reproach made her laugh for happiness.

'I give you my trust,' he said. 'What more could I give? It's my best.'

She looked at him straightly and earnestly. Then she went close to him and held her face that he might kiss her.

'God grant we never fail each other,' he said, holding her in his arms and gazing down into her eyes. 'But, Cynthia,' he added after an instant's thought, 'remember life may fail any time. If it were I, mourn and then be happy again in this world's possessions. Think of another who might want you.'

'Oh, Lucius, I never could,' she said, trembling into tears. She touched him inexpressibly.

'What, in the name of Heaven, have I done to deserve her?' he thought. Was this the meaning of the discipline of years, this the hidden leaven of good in the bitter old grief? Had he indeed been in training, as so many good souls would believe, not only for her but for happiness? Perhaps, had happiness been his when a young man he would have abused it, not recognising its value or realising its responsibilities. By this time it might have flown, unappreciated, until its eternal possibilities of good for himself and others were out of his power. Whereas he had reached the prime of his years before it was entrusted to him, and now he felt that he knew what to do with it.

It was that same day that Cynthia consented to hasten the wedding.

She told Mrs. Hennifer the next morning. Mrs. Hennifer was delighted. She had been an admirable chaperon, always at hand, yet always unseen, or if necessarily visible, abstracted. Yet she had seen, and observed, and drawn her own conclusions. She had been astonished at the influence Danby quietly and imperceptibly gained over Cynthia, but still more by the way she expanded under it. It was true indeed that he had won her. He had touched a very deep chord in her nature; its vibration was giving her that charm of charms in women, a good presence, so pervasive as to be felt even when silent, unseeking, unself-conscious. She was becoming fond of Danby herself. Marriage with him no longer seemed derogatory for Cynthia. It was certain he cared so little elsewhere that Mrs. Severn could never flatter herself he cared at all. And Mrs. Severn had kept so quiet, been so thoroughly unobtrusive upon Danby's movements, that she was even in a good humour with her. She had sounded Anna on the point from time to time, and could have sworn they had never met. She was sure Cynthia would have told her had she met her when with Danby, for she had made her promise to do so. As for Anna, she knew nothing. A misgiving she had once had as to the wisdom of her ignorance was lulled. Everything had arranged itself for the best. There did not appear one little cloud upon the horizon.

But they did not all go up to town together. The rush of preparation involved more than dressmaker's and milliner's work. The Hall was to be re-decorated during their absence. Cynthia could not bear the old time-worn treasures scattered through the rooms to be left to servants. She persuaded Danby to leave them. Then she made her farewell visits and superintended the dismantling of the house.

During these few weeks the obligation of one visit was never off her mind. She hesitated, reasoned with herself, and each time she thought she had decided, found herself forget it in the ever fresh array of pros and cons.

She would not have hesitated but for Mr. Severn and Anna. She feared to wound them by leaving without having been to Old Lafer. True, she could make an excuse and send for Anna to lunch, and see Mr. Severn at home. But she detested excuses. If she did not go Mrs. Severn too might attribute some mean motive of jealousy or malice to her. Of these she was innocent. But she could not forget Hartas Kendrew's gibe; she shrank from her too as having wronged Danby, and loathed the idea of the degradation of an ill-regulated mind and uncurbed desire.

In the end she decided to go. She was condemning her on so despicable a testimony, one that might be prompted by nothing but personal spite, that she went as her only chance of reparation.

She did not drive, but walked alone

through the woods on a day so warm that their shade was delicious.

After crossing the stile before the house she found Elias on the flags, weeding between the bosses of stonecrop in their joints. He was always careful not to disturb the stonecrop because Anna was 'rare and bigoted' of it. He looked up but scarcely nodded. His personal position with regard to Miss Marlowe was an independent one; he was in Mr. Severn's service, and neither servitor nor 'tinnent' of hers. This gave him a vantage ground from which to judge her. He had judged her and disapproved of her 'courses.' His theory that the Admiral's death in the nick of time was a makeshift of Providence's to re-install the Canon as her lover, had brought him to dishonour in Dinah's estimation, for it had failed. Here she was on the very eve of marriage with a 'foreigner'! He wondered she had the 'front' to come near Old Lafer. A decenter woman would have kept herself quiet when she was demeaning herself so, and flying in the face of the best chance of mending her ways that Providence could have given her.

'Is Miss Hugo in?' said Cynthia, in passing, as she daintily lifted her skirts out of the way of soil and weeds and skep.

'Ay,' said Elias. 'And Clo—t' missis—is out.'

'Not busy, I hope—Miss Hugo?'

'Not that I kens on.'

'I thought I saw her hat above the wall as I came up the fields.'

'Maybe you did.'

'She has been gardening too, perhaps?'

'Nay.'

'Was it her?'

'Ay.'

'Is she there now?'

'Nay,' said Elias, taking up his skep and moving on.

'Thank you,' said Cynthia. She was sincerely grateful for the amusement he had given her.

'I'm none particler as to thanks,' said Elias slowly and imperturbably. 'If you want my thanks you'll get 'em by stepping up to t' house in a *decorous* way.'

'Certainly,' said Cynthia involuntarily. She was so much startled that she went on hastily, and did not venture to laugh until she was in the parlour. Then she astounded Anna by bursting into a merry peal that left her breathless.

'Wonderful old man! Lucius must know him!' she exclaimed, when she had mimicked both words and tone.

'I thought *we* should have known Mr. Danby by now,' said Anna.

Cynthia had just settled herself on the sofa, throwing herself back to rest. But at this she suddenly sat upright.

'You don't mean to say that you don't

know him?' she said, with dawning certainty that this was the fact.

'I have not seen him. You never brought him here and I never met him. He was always at the Hall, and I never was, except at Christmas, when we did not happen to meet.'

'Oh dear!' said Cynthia.

She became silent. Assuredly she had not taken him to Old Lafer, and what was more, she did not intend to. As it was not probable he would go without her, he would never go. She was convinced from Anna's manner that she, and possibly also Mr. Severn, had commented on their absence as singular and unkind. In her regret she unconsciously misled her.

'I fear we have been very selfish and self-absorbed,' she said. 'You must forgive us, Anna. Really, I have introduced him to no one, being so quiet you know, and not visiting at all. I fear I have forgotten my duty. It must seem strange to you.'

'Never mind,' said Anna; 'it will really be more interesting to welcome him as Mr. Danby-Marlowe.'

'Yes,' said Cynthia.

'And you won't be very long away, will you?'

'No,' said Cynthia. She felt paralysed, and as monosyllabic as Elias. How far and how deep were these results to penetrate?

Anna thought her preoccupied, but that was natural. She was paler than usual too, but evidently she was tired. She was so conscious of looking pale herself, and wishing to escape remark, that she passed over any shortcomings of Cynthia's with trepidation. She rang for tea and sat down with her back to the light. Neither had she taken off her hat. She was thankful that she happened to be wearing it; it gave natural shadow to her face.

Cynthia looked round the room. Now that she found herself here she was conscious of indescribable feelings. She glanced at Anna, associating her with Danby's youth. A violin and guitar with music lying open spoke eloquently of Mrs. Severn, and her object in having broken faith with Danby. Yet it was not so much of the wrong done as of herself that Cynthia now thought. There was a photograph of her in her handsome maturity on the mantelpiece. Her baby, Mrs. Marlowe's god-child, lay in the cradle Anna was rocking. She got up and went and looked at the baby that bore her grandmother's name. As she looked she fancied that Anna was gazing at her strangely. She had an odd feeling of impersonality, as though she were losing her identity, and becoming absorbed into Mrs. Severn's. Surely, too, it was impossible that no one knew how or why she was here to-day, and had not been before, and would not come again.

Would not come again! No, Lucius should not come, that was the fact. Herself she would not excuse, but she would always find excuses for him. After all, was she jealous? Was this what that maddening rush of blood over neck and face meant? But if she were jealous it was certain she did not fully trust. Was that before her, a struggle with the demon of distrust? When her husband was not with her, would she wonder where he was? Would it ever impel her to walk to Old Lafer to assure herself that Mrs. Severn was at home, and that Danby was where he had told her he was going, or at least not there?

She rose, clasped her hands, then flung them apart with the old girlish gesture, and walked to the window. She felt as though there were bandages at her throat which she must tear away before she could breathe freely.

'Where is your sister?' she said.

'Walking with the children,' said Anna.

'*Out!*' said Cynthia. She turned and looked at her, then, conscious that her eyes must express more desperation than she had allowed to her voice, she smiled, and returning to the sofa, sat down as much in the shadow as possible.

'Why not *out?*' said Anna, smiling too. Cynthia's smile had struck her as forced and miserable, and now hers struck Cynthia as the same. Their eyes met, and they looked at each other fixedly, each recognising inquiry and knowledge in the other. But what knowledge? Each rapidly reviewed her own, and was convinced that it could not be known to the other. They must be mistaken, and were only rousing mutual suspicions. Cynthia tore her eyes away, and mastered herself into conventional indifference.

'She used never to be out,' she said; 'at least not beyond the pastures or her hammock in the garden. I never remember her being out when I have called here. Has she become fond of walking?'

'Yes, I think she has.'

'And leaves you here as nursemaid? I suppose if she were to become fond of staying in again she would not ask you if you cared to walk.'

'Oh dear, no! But why should she? She knows I care for it,' said Anna naïvely.

Again Cynthia was silent. She saw she had spoken in perfect good faith and without sarcasm. So Mrs. Severn had developed vagaries, and probably would make the household miserable if they were not gratified. She forgot herself so far for one moment as to put her hand to her head and hold it while she thought. But she could not think. She only said to herself again and again, 'Why did I come here?' Anna could think. She rocked the cradle, and while watching the sleeping baby, her thoughts bore her into a groove of inexpressible sadness. One might have seen that her eyes had the sombre and fathomless depth of a hidden grief constantly brooded over, and that her lips would readily tremble not at chiding, but at sympathy.

Peggy now brought tea in, and over it the tension on their spirits relaxed. Anna exerted herself to be lively. She was only anxious that Cynthia should not lengthen her visit, she wanted her to miss Mrs. Severn. Cynthia, however, was debating within herself whether she would do so or not. She wanted to see her, yet dreaded it, fearing that knowledge might prejudice her, and either irritate or abash Clothilde. Yet, it was so long since she had seen her that she felt certain that she could judge in a moment as to the ravages vice would make or might have made. She knew how few women can become debased and not show it. If it were to be Mrs. Severn's fate, she might dismiss this vague horrible fear of her as a factor for misery in her own life at once and for ever. Her indefinite consciousness of dread had now taken form. She acknowledged to herself that it was the faint hope of this possibility that underlay the cruel vividness of Hartas Kendrew's words. Shame of it had made her conscience-stricken, and kept her from taking Mrs. Hennifer into confidence. Despicable though it was she could not have expressed sincere sorrow. She too was falling. What would Danby think of her if he could see into her heart now? And yet it was her love that was her temptation; she could not endure to think that its fruition of mutual joy was in a moment's jeopardy. Surely Mrs. Severn was not to have the power of again embittering Danby's life.

When at last she rose to go, Mrs. Severn had not returned. She had stayed so long that she now told herself it was not intended that they should meet. Perhaps, indeed, she was walking with the purpose of avoiding her, having thought she might come. She was leaving Lafer to-morrow, this was her last day, as every one knew. She had said all to Anna that she had to say, and entrusted one or two pensioners to her care. Kit Kendrew was the first of these. He was better now, but she was particularly wishful that he should be even stronger than before his imprisonment, that he might do her full credit. This she said, then laughed, shamefacedly. She had taken Anna's arm as they went through the hall, and now they stood together on the top of the steps in the full sunshine.

'Really, though, that is not my only reason,' she said. 'His father cursed me and mine, I want him to moderate his bitterness. What woman would be strong enough to bear curses and threats of revenge just when life was opening out to her by marriage?'

'What woman would?' said Anna, 'when

it was no longer her own life only that was involved? I should be strong enough to break the new tie, but not to drag one I loved above the whole world and myself into the curse too.'

She spoke in a low tone of intense feeling. The tone struck Cynthia even more than the words or her acquiescence. It was personal. She was not sympathising. She was speaking out of an emotion that stirred her to her heart's core, and was the bitter fruit of some terrible individual experience. Cynthia looked closely at her.

'Anna, when are you going to be married?' she said.

The question escaped involuntarily the instant it flashed into her mind or she would not have uttered it.

Its effect electrified her. Anna became deadly pale, her eyes dilated and glowed with a fire that yet suggested a hoard of unshed tears. Then she pulled her arm away from Cynthia's and buried her face in her hands.

Cynthia was shocked.

'My darling girl,' she said, drawing her within the house again, then caressing her, 'I had no right to ask such a thing, none. I am becoming unutterably thoughtless and selfish. I had no idea that you had any trouble. But it will pass, Anna, and the sun will shine again. There are often misunderstandings, but the understanding is the sweeter and completer afterwards. When people truly love each other, all must come right. And I am convinced that he does love you,' she added in a whisper.

Anna's hands fell, but there was no smile on her face. It was sombre and hopeless.

'It is my doing, Cynthia,' she said.

'Yours?' said Cynthia.

'Yes, wholly. He won't take it. He is goodness itself to me.'

'But, Anna, are you fully justified? Are

you arguing from some mistaken sense of duty? You can't mean that you have broken your promise.'

'He will not listen——'

'Of course he will not. Is it likely when you have not changed towards him? He will know how to overcome every difficulty.'

'Cynthia, don't! You will break my heart,' cried Anna sharply. 'He must believe me! Far from marrying him this spring as he asked, I don't know whether I can ever marry him, not for years. And is it right that I should let him wait? Oh, it is hideous! Don't ask me what it is. But I am in trouble, real, deep, hard trouble; it's hardening me. I can't see the end. There's only one thing worse than the present, that is the future. And such a little while ago all was so bright!' she said passionately.

Cynthia was silent. She could not ask for her full confidence when it was thus withheld. She knew too now that in all probability there was nothing to tell which she did not know. But to have inferred this would have been another wrench at the wound.

'Heaven forgive the weak woman who is making all this misery,' she thought. Then she took Anna in her arms and kissed her.

'I am going to joy and I leave you to grief,' she said. 'But only God knows in which the truest blessing lies. Besides which our cases may soon be reversed. But, Anna dear, *be still*. Take the sorrow as your own, but throw yourself into every interest for others yet. Take the sorrow to God and wait for His light to shine into it. Then you will see your way out of it.'

They went back to the front door and there they parted. Cynthia, however, stood a moment at the bottom of the steps and looked up at Anna.

'I think we shall go round the world for our honeymoon,' she said.

Anna could not forbear smiling. She thought the joke was coined to amuse her, having no clue either to Cynthia's train of thought or to her logic.

But it was not a joke.

CHAPTER IV

ANNA FACES THE SITUATION

'AND so you had Miss Marlowe to-day?' said Mr. Severn that evening at tea. 'I was just crossing the park from the lake and met her coming out of the wood. I told her we all thought she'd forgotten us. It never once seemed to have entered her mind that you would have cared to see Danby. She only remarked that it was most odd you never had seen him when he had been about so much.'

'I did not see Miss Marlowe; I was out,' said Mrs. Severn.

'It was her last day; I wonder you did not stay in.'

'I did not care to see her.'

'A most excellent reason, alias an inexcusable one, my dear woman. It seems that had she not come, what I should have resented you would have rejoiced at. Well, had she not come, she would have sunk several degrees in my estimation. I wonder she did not say she had not seen you.'

'She saw Anna. You had a long talk, hadn't you, Anna?' said Mrs. Severn, turning and looking curiously at her. She was certain that when she came in from her walk Anna's eyelids showed traces of tears, and had pondered over the wisdom of her tactics in having left them to meet alone. Was it possible that either had told the other anything, or that each had told all?

'Yes, we had a long talk,' said Anna. 'She is a good woman; I hope she'll come back as she goes.'

'She means to give herself time to change, eh?' said Mr. Severn. 'Never knew anything so preposterous as this chevy round the world. I declare such whirligigs make my sober old head dizzy. I always feel as though the Equator were a greased tram-line when I hear the equanimity with which folks discuss such a journey. And for the air with which she announced it she might have been talking of driving into Wonston.'

'Why, Dad, she named it to me, but I took it for jesting.'

''Twas serious earnest, my honey.'

'What do you mean?' said Mrs. Severn, looking from one to the other. 'Is the wedding put off? You did not tell me, Anna.'

'I told you nothing,' said Anna. 'What we said would not have interested you.'

''Tis the honeymoon,' said Mr. Severn. 'Nothing under a year will satisfy her. Danby is to be her greased tram-line, telegraph, pay, write, arrange every luxury and convenience for inscribing their names in every hotel visitors'-books in the five continents, *via* three oceans. Heaven knows where a genuine business letter will ever find them! What can have hatched such a wild-goose chase?'

'If it is her doing he will probably put his veto on it,' said Mrs. Severn.

'Not a bit of it; I fear quite the other way. He worships her. He can't thwart her when the wherewithal too is hers.'

'Perhaps it is only a whim,' said Anna.

'She's not a whimy body, Anna, or I should have seen no danger ahead myself. No, when I came upon her she was walking with her eyes on the ground, and when she looked up her smile was heavy with deep studying, and she just said her say and then she bid me tell you she'd write now and again, and would you, and the old bridge was to be finished by they got back. It looks to me as if Danby were going to make her into a gad-about, and if he does 'twill be a sad day for Lafer when they wed. But she's so fond of

Lafer I can't believe she'll turn her back upon it.'

He got up as he spoke and walked to the window, thrumming on the pane and softly whistling. They all knew these as signs of distress of mind rather than of lightheartedness. In fact he could not bear to think of Lafer Hall being empty. It was bad enough for the wedding not to be there. That it should be closed for a year, filled him with uneasy presentiment. He clung to custom and detested change. Association had a potent charm for him. Every day of his life he regretted Danby's advent, and vehemently wished that Tremenheere was to be the future master. He had no clue to that mood of Cynthia's which would have left her unmarried had she not met the one man who could win her. Thus he failed to realise the security of her happiness, and allowed prejudice to bias him against her choice.

He stood a long time looking out, his eyes

fixed upon the haze of smoke in the distance that hung above Wonston. The town was not visible from here; East Lafer interposed on slightly higher ground. When he turned no one but Anna was left in the room and she had sat down to some work. He looked at her a moment with a scrutiny of which she was unconscious, then called her.

'Come here,' he said.

When she obeyed, rising more readily in her abstraction than she would have done had she been thinking, he put his hand on her shoulders and held her, looking down at her.

She looked up at him. His face was dear to her. It had become much dearer since Christmas. The ageing of its lines, the fading of its ruddy health, the graying of his hair, all were seen and idolised with passionate love and grief. She knew, and Dinah knew, that it was not the Admiral's death that had worked the change. Their self-reproaches came too late. When he flung Dinah aside and rushed upstairs to know the worst, when he found his wife abandoned to her dreadful imbecile stupor, the iron entered into his soul, the joy of life was quenched in him for ever. Dinah knew it. Anna had only to come home to know it too.

His smile at her now forced tears to her eyes, it was so sombre.

'Anna,' he said. 'Tell me what's the matter with every one. Nothing's going as it seems to me it was meant to. Why is Miss Marlowe going to the ends of the world? Why did Clothilde avoid her to-day? What's the matter with you? What's got Geoffry Borlase? Ay, ay, you think I'm buried in business, but for all that I'm not an automaton or a mummy. I can see and hear and think. What is it, Anna lass—a lover's quarrel?'

'Do you want me to leave you?' said Anna with a faint smile but a steady voice. 'Don't you think it will be better for every one if I wait until Antoinette is grown up?'

'But Borlase, my honey? When he spoke to me he said he'd be his own master this year, and he looked to claim you then.'

'Antoinette will only be at school two years and she goes at midsummer.'

'But you didn't hang back on that when you passed your word.'

'I don't hang back now, Dad.'

'Then who does? Tell me the truth, Anna.'

'Still if any one does, it is I,' she said, faltering in a way that he considered unaccountable in her.

''Tis Borlase!' he exclaimed sharply. 'You are beating about the bush. You want to shield him——'

'No,' she said. 'He thinks as I do.'

He dropped his hands, and moving from her leant against the shutter and looked at her with astonishment.

'He's ready to wait two years?' he said slowly. 'That makes him into a lukewarm lover on the top of your promise, and by

George he hasn't the air of one! Have I to take your word, my lass? I'm loath to, and still I'd be loather to think I'd to square him in his duty. Is it the truth that you've talked it over and come to this plan? Is it your plan, Anna; or is it his for a makeshift to put it all off bit by bit, and leave you in the lurch in the end. Anna, my lass, is he shamed of us now?'

His eyes seemed to pierce her. Then his voice sank. He turned away and looked out of the window unseeingly.

She could not speak for a moment. She had dreaded this, and yet it took her by surprise. A sob thickened in her throat; she gulped it down and smiled.

'No, he is not,' she said. 'Dad, don't you know Geoff better than that? What he knows I told him, because it was right to tell him. Dad, shall I tell you what he did? He took me in his arms. He kissed me. He told me he would wait so long as I chose.

He will never marry any one but me. But it is I who have to name the wedding-day; not you, remember, dear Dad.'

He looked at her again with great fondness. She put out her hand and he took it between his own.

'Then this waiting has to be for my sake,' he said slowly. 'Anna, it goes against me. I'll none have it so. A deal that's comforting 'll go with you, my bright lass, but it belongs by right to Borlase. We'll hob-nob on without it. Dinah 'll stay. For all she and Elias worship you, they'll none desert me; death only 'll part Dinah Constantine from my fortunes since that night, Anna, when, God Almighty forgive me, I could have sent my poor wife's soul to judgment—her frail body, what was it worth——?' he stopped suddenly, gasping. Drops of sweat stood on his brow. He took out his handkerchief. She saw how violently he trembled, and pushing a chair up to him, gently forced him into it. She knelt down by him, and rested her elbows on the arm of the chair, propping her face in her hands, and looking at him with eyes that sparkled with tears.

'Dad,' she said, 'we won't talk of it. Let it rest. Try not to think of it. But Geoffry and I have thought it all out. I wanted to give him his liberty. I told him I could not leave Old Lafer until Antoinette had been to school and came home, and could keep house; and that it was not right to keep him waiting. Clothilde is my sister. I cannot forsake her. It is my place to watch over her. I can't leave her to Dinah. Neither will I leave you. It is my sister who has brought this misery on you; I'll do what I can to make up for it. No one shall know but those who do already, if I can help it. When Antoinette comes home, she must know—unless she is better then,' she added wistfully; then after a little pause she went on, 'Geoffry says she will probably never overcome it, that this vice overmasters a woman, that a man can master it, but a woman never——'

'Anna,' Mr. Severn broke in, 'if that's gospel truth, the sooner she's in her grave the better. Anna,' he said, resting his forehead on his clenched hands to hide his face, 'I don't mind telling thee;—I can't keep it from thee, may God forgive me, but I canna live with a wife who's a drunkard.'

'Good God!' said Anna involuntarily. She got up, and going to the window pressed her face against the glass to cool the burning blush that had rushed over her. She had never thought of this.

There was a long silence. Mr. Severn sat on, bent with his woe and degradation. Anna presently passed him and threw herself into a corner of the sofa. She knew not what to say. His words had been a revelation to her, had banished every possibility of mere sentimental forbearance; they were like the scalpel that raised the flesh and discovered the disease. This then was what he had brooded over; a sick loathing had been generated in his soul and now confronted him as a physical impossibility. She knew he would never have said so much had he not felt much more. She had prayed for strength to pity and not to hate. If he too had, his prayer had failed.

At last Anna spoke again, clearing her voice and steadying it with an effort.

'What do you mean to do then? Have you made any plan? Do you mind telling me?' she said gently.

'*Do? Plan?* Nay, nay, I've neither thought nor reasoned. I've only felt,' he said in a hopeless way utterly foreign to his nature.

'Do you wish me to arrange something?'

'I don't know, Anna?'

She was silent again, her spirit quenched by his loss of it.

Presently he moved wearily, with a deep

sigh. She thought he was going, and instantly sprang to her feet to stop him.

'Dad,' she said, 'let us talk it out, once for all. Tell me, have you ever spoken to Clothilde, or have you only condemned her by your silence?'

'That's all,' he said.

'And you have gone on in the old way with her, always?'

'Ay, I have; with a difference.'

'In spite of this dreadful feeling? I don't want to condone her shamelessness, but still remember how many wives have to bear with drunken husbands; the law gives them no redress for the bestiality of coming home to them in a condition of beasts, and this when it is so wanton that it cannot be considered a disease. I know it is worse in a woman, infinitely worse; but I think, so does Geoffry, that it is a disease with Clothilde. Suppose we treat it so.'

Mr. Severn laughed shortly, then groaned.

'Dipsomania,' he said, 'scientific treatment, a choice between a retreat, or allopathic doses of alcohol at home. Anna, tell me, are they paroxysmal attacks or is the craving always there?'

For a moment, in her deep distress, after one swift keen glance at him, she covered her face with her hands. Then she came and knelt down by him again and told him all.

Clothilde had fallen again, and she had found her. With the door bolted against all intruders she had watched by her in the stupor that followed. No human being could fathom the anguish of that watch. Its only relief had been in movement. She had paced the room, knowing that no sound was likely to disturb the figure prone on the sofa, whom she had had to cover with wraps, while heart and flesh revolted against the contact. She bent every resource of her reason to the possibility of shielding Clothilde, and concealment from Mr. Severn. The task was an appalling one. She could scarcely have carried it out so far but for Borlase. It was certain that Clothilde drank in secret—probable that she had done so for long. Anna had discovered that eau-de-cologne and spirits of wine served her purpose. She remembered immediately the quantities of these that had appeared in their chemist's bills, and how she had more than once rallied her on her extravagance with perfume, and a little lamp she burnt. It was, however, her only extravagance and was passed over. Borlase took her in hand as a *case*. From that time things had at once been sweeter and more bitter. His love and faithfulness were indeed a covert from the tempest, but she felt that she dragged him too in the mire. It now became certain that moods of passivity which the household had attributed to a sluggish temperament or constitutional indifference were in reality the result of some drug. Borlase told Anna that she could not do without it. Whether stimulating or cloying, her system was now to some extent dependent on it. He must discover to what extent. Enforced abstinence roused a demon of craving in her. He then ordered alcoholic doses. He trained Anna to habits of technical observation, striving to steady her nerve and balance her affection for the sinner by investing all with the interest of a scientific diagnosis.

All this Anna faithfully told Mr. Severn. It was torture to both, but they must face it. The only comfort was that they faced it together. Very comforting to him were her fondling hands, the caressing pitying tones of her voice. She did not hope to dissipate his repugnance, rather she feared she must increase it. But her principles of right were at stake. Who, knowing part, had so much claim to know all as Clothilde's husband? Her own shock at his shrinking she had conquered. But she must plead with him to further her own and Borlase's efforts.

'Surely you won't refuse to watch too, to try to save her from herself?' she said at last.

He was leaning back now, his head resting against the chair, his eyes fixed upon the sky as he looked beyond the window.

'Ay, we'll all try,' he said solemnly. 'I'll tell you what we'll do, Anna, and you must tell her—you must tell her I know all, *all*. We'll give her the year of this honeymoon to try for herself too. If it betters her, we'll forget and forgive. If it worsens her, she must go. She must go for the children's sakes. They'll know what she is. They shall not see too. She shall leave me. And maybe I'll give up my post and leave Old Lafer, and we'll go where we're none known, for the children's sakes.'

Suddenly, as he stopped, a light of anger shot into his eyes. She felt him shudder.

'God Almighty grant it's none in the bairns,' he said. 'I've been deceived, ay, I have. If Jack takes to evil courses, what can I say? Anna,' he added in a shaken voice, as she put her hand in his in silent sympathy, 'there's a knowledge that's devil-bred, and there's an ignorance that's devil-hid. 'Tis a sad thing when we learn them from a woman.'

CHAPTER V

AFTER STORM, CALM

LATER they went into the garden. It was a favourite amusement of Mr. Severn's to watch the bees and pick the daring weeds from the crannies in the mossy old wall that were sacred to rue and polypody and crane's-bill. The hawthorns round the larch planting beyond were in full flower, seeming to border its velvety green with miniver. In the meadows the dimply hollows, like elbow dents in a pillow, were flushed with the soft pink of the dock, which showed delicately in the low evening light. The shadows were lengthening. The murmur of the beck grew more distinct. The blue peat-reek hung above the wood where the cottage nestled unseen. A full moon was rising in the clear arch of sky, against which the moors lay dense and sombre.

But this balmy peace stifled Anna. She had gone out with Mr. Severn because he asked her to do so. Once, there was nothing she had enjoyed more than to saunter with him from hive to hive, and from flower to flower, smelling the lilies, discussing the larkspurs and peonies and potentillas, the damask roses and plots of herbs, or pacing up and down the flags among the golden bosses of stonecrop, talking over the interests of the day, or waxing poetic over the loveliness of earth and heaven. But to-night Mrs. Severn joined them. She was vexed because she had trailed her dress over the grass and damped it, yet was indisposed to go in. She had glanced at her husband and noticed his gravity. He did not relax, and she wished to disarm him. She thought she would hear more about Danby and Cynthia from him than from Anna. Anna left them and ran down the fields into the wood. She felt jarred and fretted.

But not long now. Soon the balmy quiet sank into her soul. For those who love nature there is compensation for woe in her readiness to be hugged to the breast of all human suffering. She has moods that soothe by sympathy, or nerve by vigorous contrast. The divining ray that elucidates pain is to be found in watching the sky, the shifting of light and shade, the blues of the distance, the colouring of field and hedgerow. Apart from their individual loveliness, all go to make the 'perfect whole' of simplicity, which is dear to the purest breeze and sunshine striking from the blue of Heaven, the void of space. Those who have the faith to face her with their loads of unrest and rebellion will not find her fail. To walk towards the sunset, or in the front of a keen air, with the intention of the colour and keenness assimilating with your emotions, is a moral tonic. It gives that which is equivalent to the most spiritual of religions.

And Anna felt this to-night. From a pent-up cry of 'How hard life is!' she gradually merged into gratitude that she lived it here, at Old Lafer with its hills and moors, its streams and woods and fields, where nature seemed to be vested in God, and God in nature. The twilight, drawing its veil over the mouldings of the landscape, and leaving only its outlines, was not only solemn but serene. The moon, rising higher, laid over this a soft suffusion that began to fill up the picture again with vague and melting shadows. Pulses seemed to throb that were unsuspected in the daytime, yet made the silence deeper. Beautiful, delicious silence, through which ran the murmur of the beck, hushed too!

She waited until the moon glimmered on the water. It lay like silver flakes here and there up the gill betwixt the overarching of oak and alder. Above, on the ridge of the pastures, the old house loomed in dense shadow, but the moors beyond were already overspread with the glow that linked them to the night, as they were never linked to the day. Subtly sweet was this mood wherein Earth seemed to rest herself against Heaven.

Presently she left the bridge and went into the wood. But there was no need now to walk fast. Passion was already exorcised. She had not only seen and heard, but felt what the eventide had for her. It was now part of herself, and she was so much the better woman than she had been an hour before. What comes thus may make us breathless at first by reason of the very fulness of the measure, but it never leaves us. It is the rift in the clouds through which the sun-ray streams into the very heart of the chosen ground.

She walked until she came to the edge of the wood, where a stile led to the path that bisected the one from the Mires. The park with its encircling plantations, the hollow where the lake lay, every undulation, the slope trending downwards from the bowling-green and the terrace, were distinctly modelled in the moonlight. The house gleamed white, except where the cedars at the corner facing her threw a blotch of shadow. There were lights in the library and some of the upper windows. Probably Mrs. Hennifer and Cynthia were finishing their packing. She was almost certain that the blinds were not drawn down; already the house showed its dismantled condition, and suggested a state of confusion and hurry. She had a great longing to see Cynthia again. She felt that the old Cynthia was going away for ever. Mrs. Danby-Marlowe would be some one different, a creature whom she would have to learn to know, and on whom the old impressions might sit awkwardly. She too resented the idea of prolonged and indiscriminate travel for her; she might leave a bit of herself here and another bit there, and come back a patched-up or remodelled marionette. Anna had strong insular prejudices. England and home were precious and significant words to her. And Cynthia Marlowe, so bright, so artless, so buoyant, had been so English and so homelike, that it seemed desecration for her to dispose of herself all over the world by rushing trains and throbbing steamers. She little knew that six hours before Cynthia herself would have been the last to propose such a journey. She had told Danby she would not want to be long away from Lafer. As she rose from lunch that day she had said to herself that they would return in two months' time ready for the grouse over the dogs on the twelfth. And now she was resolved to be gone a year at least. In that time surely it would be cure or kill at Old Lafer. But she had not told Mrs. Hennifer yet. She would tell her nothing until she had told Danby, and her reasons he only should know.

She was not in the house to-night. The maids were packing. She had thrown a shawl on and gone out to the terrace. But for the interposing cedars Anna would have seen her there, standing against the balustrade with her eyes fixed upon the middle-distance where the lights of Wonston twinkled. Slightly to the left of the town thus shown, the Minster stood. Its nave was illuminated. It was this fact that had attracted Cynthia and then glued her to the spot where she stood. It flashed into her mind that this was Ascension Day and Anthony Tremenheere, when he came to bid her good-bye, had told her that he was the evening preacher. He had almost asked her to be there. And she had meant to be. Then she had never thought of it again. Her mood of tender reminiscence became strongly dashed with self-reproach. He would look for her in the Deanery pew where she always had a seat. He would think she had sacrificed the old friendship. She could not bear this thought.

Anna, still gazing from the stile, suddenly saw a tall and slender figure emerge from the cedars and flit round the house towards the stables. She thought it was a maid, though the figure was like Cynthia's.

'If I could be sure it were her,' she said to herself, 'I would go and have another kiss. But she'll be busy.'

And with that she turned away and plunged again into the eerie wood. It was like her to be thus literal. Herself romantic rather than sentimental, she overlooked the possibility of Cynthia being overpowered to-night by thoughts of the past and its associations, rather than buoyed up by the fulfilment of happiness that was impending.

But Cynthia had flitted round to the stables with a purpose. She came across one of the grooms immediately and ordered the horses to be put into the carriage. She was going down to Wonston.

She told Mrs. Hennifer, but did not ask her to go with her.

'I shall not stay talking,' she said. 'But since I forgot him so completely I shall go and tell him. He will forgive me then, and it won't wound him so much.'

'Unless it wounds him more,' thought Mrs. Hennifer. No man who had loved her could see those innocent clear eyes of Cynthia's pleading for forgiveness for such a self-confessing fault without an awakening of the old yearning. But some pain is exquisite. They who have loved worthily dare let themselves love on.

'And you don't mind going alone? It is late,' said Mrs. Hennifer.

'I don't mind at all. It's only like going out to dine.'

'But to Anthony's?'

'No. Why should I?' then struck by an after-thought, she added, 'Don't you think it's quite proper? You should say so. You know I never see an insinuation. But why isn't it? If the servants wonder they will be certain it's business. For myself, I'm sure it is the right thing to do. Anthony knows me.'

When she reached the Close the Minster was dark.

'Its lights are out,' said Cynthia to herself, leaning forward and looking at it as they rolled past. 'Well, that does not matter. But it would matter very much if I extinguished one spark of light in Anthony's life. No, he shall not think badly of me. I let him be sure I should be at service to-night.'

The carriage stopped at his house. She got out and stepped under the verandah with its hanging sprays of virginia creeper. Yes, the Canon was at home. She followed the servant across a hall lined from floor to ceiling with books and up the stairs. He raised a heavy velvet curtain and rapped at the door of the library. A voice answered 'Come in.'

She went in, the door was instantly closed, and she was left standing just within the room.

It was a long low room with three windows down one side. At the first glance it too seemed to be furnished entirely with books. They not only lined the walls, but low tiers of shelves protruded between each window towards its centre. A finely-carved oak mantelpiece was at one end. In front of it, facing a window, was the writing-table. Japanese bronzes and magnificent specimens of Benares brass work, genuine lacquer cabinets, ivories from China and vases of jade, soap-stone, and lapis lazuli, mosques carved in sandal-wood, silver statues of Buddha, pagodas in mother-of-pearl, choicest Oriental china and inlaid Persian metal-work, gleamed from every bracket and shelf caught by the moonlight that streamed through the uncurtained windows. Their effect against the time-worn calf or the more modern morocco bindings with their gold lettering, and the crimson velvet draperies, was fine in the extreme. The uncarpeted floor of dark polished oak with a Kurdestan rug spread here and there, added richness by a hint at reflection. The only picture hung above the mantelpiece. It was an engraving of Francia's 'Entombment.' Below, was a silver crucifix. The hearth was filled with palms and a white Nile lily that scented the whole room.

For a moment after Cynthia's entrance there was silence. Tremenheere had evidently not heard her name, and she could not distinguish him. She stood still, wrapped in her dark cloak, but with the hood falling back and showing her golden hair and the lovely contours of her face. All at once it struck her how late it was. She had never been in this room so late. Before it had always impressed her as that of a traveller and a scholar. Now it seemed mystic and devotional.

The moonlight fell full on the Francia, giving it a ghastly realism. She clearly distinguished the grief-swollen eyelids of Mary the Mother of Jesus. She had sometimes looked at them until she could bear to look no longer.

But where was Anthony?

She did not speak, but advanced a step or two.

And now she saw a prie-dieu betwixt the writing-table and the hearth, and before it a kneeling figure.

She stood transfixed. A vivid blush surged over neck and face, her eyes dilated, then became suffused with shame at her intrusion. She turned away instantly and went on tip-toe to the door. But with her hand on the handle she paused and looked back. She had heard a movement. He had raised his head and was closing the book on which it had rested. But it was certain he had not the least idea she was there.

He had not. He thought the servant had departed until a more convenient season, and that he was alone.

She watched him go to the window and glance out, then turn to the writing-table. She came back and stood in the moonlight.

'Anthony,' she said.

He looked up and saw her, and stood looking.

'Anthony,' she said again, and her voice trembled, 'It is only I, Cynthia. I forgot the service. I came to tell you. I thought you might have felt it unkind.'

But she was certain by now that he would

think it more strange that she should be here. Yes! the thought was in his look that never wavered from hers.

Instinctively he took up a book, and holding it endwise on the table, clutched it with both hands and leant slightly forward.

'And did you come to tell me this?' he said.

'Yes.'

'It is very good of you, Cynthia.'

'But I forgot——'

'You mean that I could not think that good of you? No, I did not. I looked for you and I missed you. But I concluded you were too fully occupied. And I knew I had wished you good-bye. I thought perhaps you considered it most kind not to be at the Minster, although I had named it to you.'

His tone chilled her, it was so measured. Yet a little cry of pain escaped her.

'Oh, Anthony,' she said, 'I see how cruel I have been now.'

She had. He did not contradict her. He could not. The scene to him was agonising. Just when he had reconciled himself to the thought that he should never again see Cynthia Marlowe, she stood before him. He could have groaned. The temptation was so poignant in its unexpectedness. He longed to take her in his arms.

Cynthia was appalled. She felt unable to move, yet to say more would only be to blunder more. His set face, unearthly pale in the moonlight, told its tale as she had never before read it. It was an insult to wish him not to care so much. A feeling more mighty than she had ever imagined held him in its grasp. She was powerless to avert or soothe. She had shattered the peace he had been wrestling for and had gained.

For a moment they still looked at each other with a fascinated mesmeric glance. Hers of bitter self-reproach thrilled him.

But his did not kindle. He maintained its steady neutrality. But every nerve and pulse in him bade her go, implored her to go.

She turned again without a word, opened the door and lifted the curtain. A clock in the hall was chiming ten. The servant came forward to the bottom of the stairs and preceded her. She stood and readjusted her cloak, drawing the hood half over her face. In that instant she felt rather than saw that Anthony was at her side.

But she could not look at him. She dreaded his farewell smile. She did not hold out her hand, and he did not offer his. She wished she had not come. She threw herself back and cried like a child with a child's question in her heart. Why must we give each other pain? Why do some love uselessly? What is the good of loving and not being loved?

Anthony, left alone, seized his hat and went into the garden. He paced up and down in the moonlight. At first his eyes were bent on the ground—earthworms that we are, how naturally do they turn there! This was while his face was troubled; while his arms still ached to have held Cynthia—oh! how closely. He was shocked and astonished with himself. To think that his dearly-won calm should have been shattered in a moment! He had never before been so conscious of human weakness. He had always had power to control his love. But she had taken him unawares. He thought of her; to have won her for his wife, what bliss it would have been. But his love was lonely. Yet he would love on. This moment's frightful passion should be conquered—nothing should be left but would bless her.

It was a struggle, but he fought it out. He must exorcise this mad longing to see her again, this darting into his mind of ways and means for doing so. She had asked him to her marriage, half hinted that he should marry her. He had refused in all purity. Was he now to debase himself by taking back his word for the sake of indulgence? He might see her at the station to-morrow. What harm in that; a moment's chat with Mrs. Hennifer standing by, a clasp of the hands? But no, it would mean more to him now. He would not see her again.

He lifted his head and stood still. The Minster rose before him, each line and curve massed by the silver shining of the moon that rode high in the heavens where no cloud drifted. The strength, the purity, the lucent air, the stillness of the dense mass against the soft sky, all touched him and lightened his heart. Yes, sorrow and joy are equally life. Who but the fool says life is not worth living? Who but the fool would have it all joy? Was he the worse for not having all he wanted? Was any one necessarily the worse for sorrow?

'Cynthia, my darling,' said Tremenheere, taking off his hat as though he were before an altar, and speaking aloud as though he wished a deity to search his heart; 'my darling Cynthia, all happiness attend you! God give you all that is good for you. God forgive our negligences and ignorances both of Him and of ourselves.'

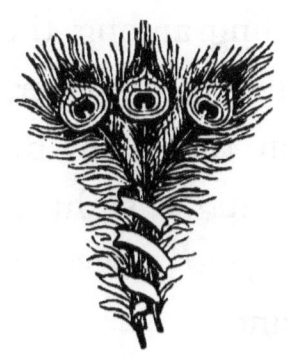

CHAPTER VI

THE RUBICON IS PASSED

SOME weeks later Anna was one day sitting on the stile into the meadows, watching Jack and Joan tumbling among the hay, when she heard Emmeline calling her, first from the hall, then from the front-door steps. She turned as she caught sight of her, and Emmeline came flying across the flags with a letter in her hand.

'It's for you; and mother says it's from Mrs. Danby,' she said breathlessly. 'And when you've read it she wants to see it.'

'Does she?' said Anna; 'I fancy everybody will.'

'I do,' said Emmeline.

'Of course.'

'Will she tell you all about the wedding, her dress, and the cake, and Lady Lavinia Russell's——'

'I'm quite sure she won't. She left that to the papers. Remember she's been married a month, Emmie, and is in Paris. Now run away and let me enjoy it first.'

'I can't run. It's too hot.'

'Then walk, saunter, creep, anything you like, only run away,' said Anna with delightful preoccupation.

Emmeline laughed; but it was also too hot for explanations, and she went off, swinging her sun-hat by its ribbons, and shaking her hair off her shoulders.

It was intensely hot and more droughty than had been known for years. The hay made itself. Scythes were sharpened at three in the morning, and the dewy swathes, once tossed, were ready for the barn at night.

Cattle, tormented by the flies, galloped madly round the pastures, and where there was no shelter, had, in one or two cases, dropped dead of sunstroke. The becks were nearly dry, leaves hung shrivelled and scorched, the landscape began to look more brown than green. Still it was delicious. Anna and the children were out all day. The ground was so dry that they could sit or lie just where they chose. The bilberries were ripe before the last cuckoo had flown. They had gone up the gill to the moors and spent hours on the bilberry beds. Sometimes they tracked a grasshopper by its drowsy chirp here and there. Sometimes they raised a brood of downy grouse. Jack and Joan would hide in the brakes of bracken, lying on their backs in the miniature forest and gazing at the hot blue sky with its sailing white clouds, betwixt the myriad slender gold stems and lacy foliage. They could see the sultry air quivering just above the ling. They dined off the rabbit-pie they had carried in a basket slung on an alpen-stock. Racing down in the evening they played spy-ho! round the peat-stacks, or had jumping matches over the edges of the dykes from which the turves were cut. Down they sank into the fibrous earth, struggling out again without their shoes, which, amid shouts of laughter, were fished up again by the more cautious ones. Never had the wild-roses been so deeply pink, or the honeysuckle so creamy. They gathered them in the gill or from the wild hedges bordering the road to East Lafer. The parlour was sweet with them. Harebells spread sheets of blue side by side with the pink haze of burnet. Ragged-robin and butterfly-orchis vied in charm with knapweed, yellow-rattle, and thistles. Emmeline would run down into the hay-fields before breakfast and pick a handful of doddering grass from the swathes. When Antoinette had gone to school she put flowers into every letter she wrote to her, until Antoinette begged her not to do so because they made her so homesick.

As Anna broke the seal of Cynthia's letter Elias came up the fields towards the stile. She jumped down to let him cross. His scythe was over his shoulder. He had been completing a heavy day's job by tidying out the nettles from the hedge-bottoms.

'Eh! Miss Anna, it's powerful hot,' he said, resting his scythe against the wall and taking off his hat. He was in no hurry. He never was. He flourished a great red handkerchief out of his pocket and wiped his bald head clear of the great beads of sweat.

'It is hot,' said Anna. 'A thunderstorm would freshen all up nicely.'

'Ay, 'twould point the fog too, but there's no sign o' thunder. T' sky has t' look o' being that tight, stretched that parchmenty-like, that one begins to think t' springs are none meant to run among t' hills ever again.

And then what's to become o' t' cattle, t' thousand hills and no kye? 'Twould be a mistake.'

Anna laughed.

'No fear, Elias! Six months hence we shall find ourselves in clouds that have lost self-control again.'

'Well, it fair caps me what's got 'em. Dinah says they're tucked away under t' earth. We speculates, Dinah and me.'

'Quite right too, Elias! We should pay our minds a poor compliment if we didn't.'

Elias looked over the clear arch of sky again and put on his hat. Then drawing close to her he said earnestly, 'I'll tell you candid out, Miss Anna, sike a season fair caps me. But it don't fright me. Dinah's that exercised it's getting on her mind. She lays it's uncanny. What do you think, Miss Anna? A thought's occurred to me. Do you think it's like that t' Almighty's drying up t' earth ready for t' consummation o' all things?'

Anna could scarcely forbear a smile. Her lips twitched. She lowered her eyes.

'Oh!' she said, 'I don't know. That's a serious thought, Elias. I don't know what to say. I don't know.'

He looked relieved, and grasped his scythe again with renewed confidence.

'Nay, nay,' he said; 'thee's right, honey. T' angels in heaven theirsels don't ken.'

Then he crossed the stile and plodded on, and Anna was at last alone for the enjoyment of her letter.

'Dearest Anna,' Cynthia wrote, 'here we are on the first stage of our travels. Great is the difference between past and present! It's all summed up in that little word, *we*. I am no longer Ego. Oh! I hope this constant duty and pleasure of thinking of and for my darling husband will make me more careful of the tastes and feelings of every one

I am thrown with! I feel as though I were just beginning to live. Before, I was of the world but not in it; an observer of the side-lights, a spectator, not an actor, waiting for my call to the stage itself. That's just what marriage does. Your Geoffry will teach you that one day; he'll bring you to the front, into the blaze of the footlights, and you'll be proud to be there and show the best that's in you for his sake.

'Lucius is so good, so fond of me, and somehow he gives me ballast. I've been a careless creature, trampling where I thought I went lightly, and crushing where I thought I gathered. I talk all out with Lucius, but he tells me not to be introspective, or I shall soon be morbid. Morbid indeed! I shall have too much to do.

'You would see our wedding in the *Morning Post*. Theo wrote me it was well reported; she sent a copy, but I hadn't time —or inclination—to read it. Lucius wouldn't let me wear my travelling dress. I had to wear white—you see he "lorded" it before it was his due. Dear old Henny said I could not look better when I am presented. "Lady Lavinia's husband" gave me away; as I went up the church on his arm and looked at Lucius, I registered a vow that *he* should never be known as "Mrs. Danby-Marlowe's husband." He has individuality and he shall keep it. Theo was very good, she did not soak her handkerchief. She said she would have done had her brother been the bridegroom. You know how inconsequent she always is. She was all the time we were shopping, and it kept up my spirits wonderfully. Then, when she saw she did, she resented it as disloyal to Anthony, and was sulky until we had to choose another gown or match one with a bonnet. As for St. John, the first thing I saw when we came out of church was St. John Kerr—he was standing against the carriage door, lighting a cigarette. He had forgotten his lady. He threw away the cigarette, though, and gave us the sweetest smile, and he actually threw the only shoe that was allowed, one of Theo's best! She was quite angry with him. I sent her a pair from Cartomier's the other day.

'We are very quiet here, chiefly looking at pictures and driving. It's intensely hot. I wear blue spectacles, but L. says they are really rose-coloured ones. I've just made him come and see "The letter L" as proof that I already wish to abbreviate him in my regard. He smiles provokingly.

'We are really going round the world, dear Anna. I proposed that we should take a yacht straight to Kamschatka where the scenery is snowy. But L. says we must do—no, *see*—we're not going to be machines—India and the States, so we join the "Rome" at Brindisi. But we are not going to hurry thither. I dread the outrageous quarrelling among the ladies in the cabins, and mean to start with cooler weather for the Red Sea. Lucius knows everything about the voyage and dislikes it for me.

'He wants me to go out now. Give love to all who ask after me, the old almshouse folk, and Scilla Kendrew, and Mr. Severn. Don't forget me to Mr. Borlase, and do go to the Hall gardens sometimes and think of the absent.—Your old friend, Cynthia Danby-Marlowe.'

She read this letter again and again. The notepaper was unscented and yet there was a perfume about it. She knew what it was, the subtly penetrating and pervading aroma of happiness. It almost seemed profane to make it free to every one. But presently she went into the garden, where Mrs. Severn was lying in her hammock, waiting for the evening breeze to bring cool comfort. She read it to her, but she said nothing, and Anna sat drowsily thinking.

She had been to the Hall the day before, and was comparing its appearance with that of previous years. The gardeners had not taken the trouble to plant out, but had sold all the cuttings. The empty beds looked inexpressibly desolate; the lawns were unmowed, their edges untrimmed. Even the greenhouses had an uncared-for look. The whole force of men was devoting its attention to the practical and profitable interests of vegetables and fruit. The house was full of workmen and decorators, its open windows seemed to gape shamelessly without their draperies of lace and brocade. She had gathered a bunch of roses that were indeed wasting their sweetness on the desert air, and then been glad to get away. She would not describe all this to Cynthia when she wrote, unless to compare it with what it would be in a year's time to welcome her home. But she thought if she knew she would command order again now.

'Anna,' said Mrs. Severn suddenly, 'let me read that letter to myself.'

She read it, then slowly replacing it in the envelope, said, 'I wonder if she meant anything when she wrote " The letter L " ? '

'Do you mean you wonder if she meant the poem, Clothilde ? '

'Yes.'

'I have no doubt she was thinking of the title ; for she puts it in inverted commas, you see.'

'I think I remember it——'

'Lazy one!' said Anna, smiling and jumping up. 'You think it would be nice to hear it read aloud now.'

'Well, you are fond of reading aloud,' said Mrs. Severn.

Anna went into the house, and returned in a few moments with a book. Sitting in the shade of the hawthorns overhanging the sweet and peaceful little garden, with the bees drowsily dipping into the lilies and snapdragons, the columbines and potentillas, she read the poem. Cynthia had thought of its title, but not of its tale.

'Lovely, isn't it?' said Anna, when she had finished. She furled the pages to and fro, and finding a certain verse, re-read it, lingering on each syllable—

> 'Shall he take much who little gives,
> And dwell in spirit far away,
> When she that in his presence lives
> Doth never stray?'

Mrs. Severn raised herself on her elbow and looked sharply at her.

'What do you mean?' she said.

'Mean? Nothing more than I say,' said Anna. 'I was thinking how different it will be with Mr. Danby and Cynthia. They each give so much, as much as possible to the other. Clothilde,' she said suddenly, 'what possessed you to scribble his name and initials on the margin of one of my books? I took down *In the Carquinez Woods*, just now, and there I saw them in your handwriting. And when did you do it?'

Mrs. Severn flushed deep red before she had time to conceal her startled agitation.

'I was reading it one day. I suppose I did so involuntarily, probably about the time of the marriage when our thoughts were full of it,' she said.

'I never saw you reading it, and I always see a gap on my shelves too, directly,' said Anna, feeling narrowly observant.

Mrs. Severn put her finger to her lip in deep thought.

'Let me see, I fancy I am wrong,' she said slowly. 'Yes, I am certain of it'—in a tone of increasing assurance—'I believe I took that book to the Mires when last I went, to read, amuse myself a little, you know.'

'Do you mean when you went, intending to stay there again, and I——'

'Yes. It was then. I remember perfectly now.'

'What nonsense, Clothilde,' Anna exclaimed sharply. 'You had never heard of Mr. Danby then. I remember perfectly, too, that it was that evening after our return that Dad told us of the engagement.'

Mrs. Severn became as pale as she had before been scarlet. She dared not glance at Anna to try to read suspicion in her expression, as she expected she should be able to do.

'Was it really?' she said feebly. 'I had forgotten. Perhaps you are mistaken as to its being my writing. I am certain I brought no book home that day; I may be wrong in thinking I took one.'

'Scilla brought it back at Christmas. Dinah told me so when I came back from the Hall after the Admiral's funeral, but I never touched it until to-day. I suppose really you must have had it out since. You left it in the ling and Hartas found it,' said Anna.

Mrs. Severn was too much frightened to

speak. She had made herself so certain that the book had never been found, that she could not trust her voice to make any further inquiry. She dared not speculate on what had become of the sheet of paper within. It was too terrifying to think that Hartas Kendrew might have appropriated that. She was very thankful that Anna allowed the subject to drop, instead of investigating it remorselessly to the confusion of all discrepancies, as she generally did a dubious point.

A few days later Anna proposed that they should all have a walk to the Mires to see Scilla, and give her Mrs. Danby's message of remembrance. Mrs. Severn had walked less lately. She said it was on account of the heat, but after an early tea it would not be so hot. The children endorsed this opinion rapturously.

'We'll go in the cool of the evening, like Adam and Eve,' said Joan to Jack.

It was a deliciously cool evening on which they went, and the moors were pleasant after the woods, which the sun never penetrated. They found all quiet at the pits. There was no sign of labour and no coalheaps. The rough shanty, crooked walls, and irregular timbers looked weirdly meaningless. A sheep ran out from a shadowy corner and startled them. The place was full of dark corners. To Anna it always suggested crime and the gallows. It seemed full of furtive, sinister eyes that watched them come and go. She had forgotten that the Mires would be deserted but for the women and children. The men would be having their equivalent of a trip to the sea or the Continent, enjoying themselves with the hay on the low-side farms, and a more generous fare than they were accustomed to at home. When they came in sight of the blue peat-reek lazily curling from the chimneys at the Mires, Mrs. Severn said she would not go into the hollow, it would be too stifling. She sat down on a hummock of ling, and the children stayed with her. Anna was afraid of the exhalations from the marsh for them. She went on alone.

Scilla was unpegging dry clothes from the line that ran across the garth, between the cottage and the stable. She put down her basket and came to meet her. Her face wore a happier look; its limpid blue eyes were less pathetic; her step was light; the curves of her lissom figure more rounded. She seemed to have said, 'Away, dull care!' and away it had flown.

'No, I'm not going to stay—at least only a moment,' said Anna, as they went indoors, and Scilla dusted a chair with her apron. 'I see Kit's good to you,' she added with a smile.

'He is that!' said Scilla. 'He's promised me he'll be content with making an honest living, and 'll never set snares again.'

'I'm afraid that will be a disappointment to Hartas?'

'I lay it is. But he puts up with it. He has to. Somehow Kit showed t' upper hand as soon as ever he began to pick up again. He said it was in his hair, like Samson. When that began to lose the gaol clip, he proved what he was made of. But I telled him it were in something different.'

'I guess,' said Anna.

'Ay; his wife's prayers,' said Scilla nodding.

'I know he'll have found out it is not good for man to be alone,' Anna said laughing. 'How often he would think of you, and what a pity it was that you were so much alone and uncared for. Perhaps he'll get work too, with these old cottages that they're going to pull down,' she added, turning and looking out to the end of the marsh where ruin and dilapidation had long reigned.

'He has already, and he will again when

he's back from the hay. I'm that lonely, but I would have him go because I thought the change o' air would just set him up to the finish. And to tell t' whole truth I'd liefer he worked at the pits. I'm none i' love with Lafer brig, neither old nor new.'

She had come and leant against the table, her fingers nervously playing with its edge. Her voice had dropped, and she looked at Anna with an air of confidential mystery and indecision.

'Why not?' said Anna. 'It will be a great deal better new than old.'

'When it's done, maybe. But I lay there'll be some mishap in the doing—at least if signs go for aught.'

'Oh, Scilla, no one believes in signs nowadays.'

'Except them that believes more, and Kit says there are sike-like who think there's a deal to learn of spirits yet. And 'twas a spirit I saw, Miss Anna. Leastways, if 'twere living woman she'd an uncanny power of making the flesh on my bones creep.'

'And when did you see it?' said Anna, with more good-humour than excitement. She perceived that Scilla was a much more self-confident and oracular person when she could quote her husband. Evidently she was now prepared to defy the world.

"'Twas three weeks ago, come Thursday. No, not the day of the wedding, or I'd have thought it boded ill for Miss Cynthy. And it wasn't her wraith neither. This was a smaller woman, smaller in length but not in girth, and she wer dark not light-complexioned, that I could take my oath on. It was as I was coming home one night. I'd been down to Wonston, doing a bit o' shopping, and I wer rather later nor I'd meant to be. Kit had promised to come and meet me under the park-walls where the road grows real lonesome, and when I went down that brant among the trees to the brig where that board of the old Admiral's shows so white, ye'll mind, Miss Anna, I wer just thinking I'd not mind gin he'd got a bit further nor t' park. Well, I turned on to Lafer brig, and my eyes clapped on a woman standing against the wall down beck. She wer on that narrow little stripe of a footpath, just where the brig peaks. I saw her clear. She had on a black cloak, one corner wer flying back, and it wer lined with white fur. And she'd a bonnet that wer black too. I never stopped. I went on, never thinking it were aught but a living soul. I wer just going to pass her with a curtsey to good-night when she wer gone. She wer clean gone, Miss Anna. 'Twer as though she'd never been on t' brig at all.'

'Oh, Scilla, you'd mistaken a tree for a figure.'

'A tree in the middle o' solid mason-work!'

'Well, its shadow then. There are trees all round, thick.'

'Ay, on either side. But there wer no moon and no shadows. It wer just i' the gloaming.'

'In fact just the hour for bogies, you would think.'

'I never thought of bogies at all. 'Twer a wraith.'

'Then do you know any one you thought it was like?'

Anna asked the question to humour her. She was startled by the intense light that sprang into her eyes. She did not answer at once, but seemed not only to take the careless question in perfect good faith but to consider that her silence must work up expectation to an exciting degree.

'You do,' said Anna. In spite of herself she felt impressed.

'I do. 'Twer a black cloak lined wi' white fur and a black bonnet. Uncommon, when they don't make a woman look as though she were i' mourning.'

'Scilla!' said Anna, starting and looking narrowly at her.

'Ay. 'Twer she, Mrs. Severn,' said Scilla slowly.

'Scilla! What nonsense! How can you tell me this?'

Scilla came close to her and took her hand and kissed it before Anna knew what she was going to do. Afterwards she continued to hold it gently as though Anna might still pull it away if she chose.

'Because I love you, ye ken I do, and she may want watching yet,' she said.

There was a little silence. Impossible for Anna to pull away her hand! and Scilla fondled it. But she little knew how divining her words had been.

'I told Kit I'd tell you, and he said 'twer right you should know. It may mean aught or naught according to your bent. But it wer that dree! I'd not tell her, if I were you.'

Anna got up.

'Oh, Scilla, I can't think it! It'll haunt me,' she said, shivering.

'I wish t' brig were done. Kit says that's t' side that's to come down, not them both because it's curious-like, and t' Admiral thought a deal of it. There, there, Miss Anna, perhaps it means naught. God Almighty kens. But there's no saying what the likes o' her may come to.'

This was poor comfort, and Scilla knew it and said no more. She went up the slope with her. Anna felt as though it were for the sake of looking at Mrs. Severn's bonnet.

'Good-by, Prissy,' said Mrs. Severn, as they started home.

Scilla shaded her eyes with one hand and watched them out of sight over the moor.

CHAPTER VII

THE REPORT OF THE BRIDE

She went slowly back to the cottage, pondering over Mrs. Severn's appearance. There might be disbelief in Anna's mind, but there was not the slightest doubt in hers as to its being a fact that she had seen Mrs. Severn's wraith. She should never forget the eeriness of the feeling that crept over her the moment the figure disappeared. She had not taken her eyes off it. From the first she thought it was Mrs. Severn, and was wondering what she was doing there alone so late. It did not move until it disappeared. Had it gone either to the right or the left she must have seen it. But it simply vanished.

At first she thought that quick as lightning it must have jumped over the parapet. The fact of standing on the narrow but rather high pathway would give strong hands leverage for such a spring. She expected to hear a cry, a splash. She ran and looked over. But there had been no sound, and there was nothing to see. Just under the arch the water gathered into a pool before flowing away again among the mossy stones. She leant far over, looking for bubbles or a ring or the rising of a figure but there was nothing.

Then she reflected that a motionless figure had silently vanished as she looked at it. Also that she had felt a queer feeling such as she had never felt before, and shuddered now to think of.

No sooner did this flash upon her with all its force than she started to run. There was not a human creature to be seen or heard, though she could discern some cattle among the brakes of bramble and ragwort. These, however, gave no secure sense of companionship. She watched the road ahead fearful of seeing that figure again before Kit met her. When at last she saw him coming leisurely along with his hands in his pocket and a short clay pipe between his teeth, power to run deserted her and she sank down on a heap of stones, calling him faintly.

After this there was nothing for it but to tell him all. Had it been daylight or she had not lost her senses or anything in fact but what it was, she vowed to herself she would not have told any human being except Miss Hugo. But she made him promise not to gossip about it, and she did not say why she had reason to fear its significance. They went back together and she described all to him. He searched among the trees, and went some distance along the banks of the river, but there was nothing to be seen or heard. They had not expected that there would be.

Had not Anna come soon she would have gone over to Old Lafer. It was a relief to her that Anna knew, but to Anna an added weight. She too pondered the whole way home and day by day. It was a long walk to the old bridge from Old Lafer, either by East Lafer and the lanes or round by the Hall, or she would have gone at once and tried to account for Scilla's vision by her own theory of a tree or a shadow. But she could not walk so far while the weather was so hot. Besides which it must not be moonlight as it now was. So she deferred the attempt, and in the end did not go at all; for after that moon the evenings shortened quickly. There would be different and unreliable effects of light and shade. Moreover, in spite of incredulity she was daunted by the idea of possibly confronting the same figure as Scilla had seen, when she knew also that she had left Mrs. Severn at home. She felt her strength might fail. She dare not tell Borlase, for he would laugh and order her bromide of potassium. And she dare not run the risk of taking Emmeline or Jack as company on such an errand. Then she heard that the old parapet was down and the strip of path gone and the work of levelling and widening proceeding quickly. This made it ridiculous to associate a catastrophe or an apparition with the bridge, changed as its character now was. Before many months passed she had ceased to dread, and had dismissed that terrible nightmare of suicide that had fastened at first on her mind with a sickening and cramping grip because she had felt it was in Scilla's too.

The quietude of the winter helped her to this. She had much less trouble with Mrs. Severn, who had lapsed to a great extent into her old ways. The daily routine, monotonous and trivial, that would have been intolerable to some women who did not make active interests even of the smallest duties, suited her. She never complained of dulness. She rarely went out unless she drove down to Wonston every week or two when Anna went shopping or marketing. She was content that Anna should judge for and decide for her, and rarely required what she did not offer. Her docility delighted Anna and perplexed Borlase. It was a phase of what he considered a disease, for which he was unprepared. He continually expected an outbreak, but it never came. Mr. Severn remarked upon her improved health, and even the children were happy with her.

The chief interest at Old Lafer that year was Cynthia's letters. Anna was astonished at the eagerness with which Mrs. Severn asked for and read them. The post-bag was naturally the excitement of the day, and foreign letters always have a charm of their own. In default of better the Rocozanne letters had so far monopolised that charm. But now, although Ambrose Piton was going to be married, they were relegated to a secondary consideration. The thin envelopes, whose diversity of stamps had smitten twinkling in and out among the trees. Now and then she caught the sound of the Minster bells. They had been ringing at intervals all day, and came with added sweetness on the uncertain evening air. She longed to wait and see Cynthia alight, herself unseen in some corner. She wanted to see her at once under this new aspect of 'the charm of married brows.' Would she prove herself married by a subtle added dignity of air and gesture? Or would she still run up the steps and flit along the terrace and play bowls with the old careless abandonment and infectious laughter?

But there was no chance of seeing her to-night, and she started home briskly. News of Cynthia awaited her at Old Lafer; for Borlase had ridden up the previous day and promised to have a glimpse of the bride at the station, and come and report upon her. Half-way through the wood she met Mrs. Severn and they strolled back together.

An hour or two must pass before Borlase could arrive, and meanwhile they were each lost in silent speculation as to how the travellers would look. After tea Anna went along the road, sauntering down the hill with its hedges sweet with wild-roses and honeysuckle, and listening for the ring of horse hoofs. She could hear these long before she could see a figure when the overhanging trees were in full foliage.

She had not long to wait. He came trotting down from East Lafer, and when he saw her waved his hand and trotted his horse the faster. Another moment and he was at her side, and dismounting, drew her arm through his with a smile.

'And now, how did she look?' said Anna.

'Well, she'd been travelling all day, you know.'

'Not only all day, but for weeks and months, Geoff.'

'Exactly. Such incessant locomotion would leave its marks on an archangel.'

'Then she is changed?'

'Changed? Dashed! However, she must have counted the cost.'

'I don't believe she ever thought how she looked.'

'Then she ought to have done. Appearances are an obligation laid on a woman. Let us shorten the period of indifference and say she's never cared since she was married.'

'Oh no! Really I can't believe it; she never could or would look a dowdy.'

'Wait and see. Perhaps if any one can tell her of the penalty she's paid, it will be you.'

'I never could, Geoff. Mrs. Hennifer may, when she comes, sometime; or Theodosia Kerr would in a moment. *She* is always spick and span, French in fact. But I didn't want Cynthia to be French. No! only just as English as when she went away. Oh, Geoff, I really am disappointed in her.'

He did not answer, but stopping a moment picked a daisy from the grassy margin of the road. It was already closed, but he furled back the pink-tipped petals until the golden stamens showed, then allowed them to fall back again.

'Anna,' he said, 'I don't want you "to give way to tears" as the novels say, so I'll tell the truth like a man and a Briton. You see this daisy? Well, I'm no poet, but I swear this is what she reminded me of as she stood upon the platform. Just as fresh and fair! She had on a white cloak, and I'm convinced there was pink about her headgear or her parasol; and when she got into the carriage and they drove off, the sun glinted on her hair like gold. In fact, she looked what she is, a most lovely woman.'

Anna was almost speechless from relief.

'And did she walk beautifully, just as buoyant, you know?'

'Beautifully, on my honour. And what's more I heard her voice. She spoke to me and sent her love to you, and you are to go and see her to-morrow—see *us*, she said.'

'Delightful! How good of her!' said Anna.

Borlase had not time to put up his horse to-night, so they turned and she went back with him.

'And now what about Rocozanne?' he said.

'Well, I must go. I've heard again both from Uncle Piton and Ambrose, and there's a formal invitation from Josephine, the bride-elect you know, and they won't hear of my declining. Apart from the wedding, I have not been for so long. And Ambrose wants me to stay with Uncle Piton while they are away. And really I should not know what to say in excuse. I think I might safely leave Clothilde. She is so much better, and Antoinette will be at home for her holidays.

She is very thoughtful, and I might say sufficient to her to make her very careful.'

'Yes, by all means. She'll have to know sometime,' said Borlase. 'Well now, Anna, I've been thinking those Jersey people might send me an invitation too.'

'You don't mean that you would go, Geoff?'

'Not go? Why not? I want my holiday, and I can't think of anything jollier than another man's wedding—put me in form for my own, you know; lots of champagne, et cetera. Just give them a hint and you'll see if I don't take it. I'll stay at St. Helier's, or St. Aubin's, or St. Brelade's, whichever of the saintly trio you choose for me, and we'll do the Island together. I declare it'll be like our honeymoon, a year in advance, the earnest of it, eh? Only a year now, Anna.'

'But we won't go there again, then,' she said naïvely.

'No, we won't. We'll haunt "fresh woods and pastures new." You shall choose.'

'No, you must.'

'Well, we'll both choose. Perhaps on the whole, it is my turn.'

'Your turn? We've taken no turns, have we?'

'Haven't we? You have though, you've chosen me.'

She blushed and smiled at his ardent gaze.

'Oh, Geoff,' she said, 'you put things so prettily, you might be a woman!'

He laughed joyously.

'Anna, my darling girl,' he said, 'if you put things so artlessly you'll be the death of me from delight. Now go home and write to Rocozanne. I would not have let you go, you know, if Ambrose had not got engaged. I'm certain he's going to get married first out of sheer spite, and I'd like to know him as I'm master of the situation.'

CHAPTER VIII

MEETINGS AND A MISS

CYNTHIA was on the terrace when Anna got to Lafer the next day. As she came round the cedars from the bowling-green, she was just stepping out of one of the library windows. But she did not see her at once, for she stopped and stooped to smell a saffroni rose. In that moment Anna saw she was all and more than her fancy had pictured her. She wore a white cambric dress cut loose and low round her throat. A bunch of carnations was in the waist-band. Her golden hair, dressed in a simple heavy knot, was brushed straight back from the brow, yet seemed to frame her face. And that face was not only of a warmer richer tint, but had gathered a matured charm of sensibility. It was full of expression, mirrored every thought of her own, and had perception for those of others. Anna felt there was a keen kind scrutiny in the lovely dauntless eyes, where reflection seemed to underlie observation, and brood like shadow in a mountain tarn far beneath the play of light on the surface.

But later, she found that she was changed, as buoyant but not so impulsive. Her opinions were experimental, no longer trenchant. Now and then there was a dainty imperiousness in her air. Evidently she had utterly lost the girlish sense of life's issues as hazardous, and seemed to have flung herself without reserve upon the confidence of their being decided, and answering her highest expectations.

When she saw Anna her face glowed

with happy smiles, she ran up to her and opened her arms. They kissed each other again and again.

'Oh, Anna,' she exclaimed, 'this is worth coming home to, indeed! Old friends, what can be more delightful? I had no idea until yesterday that I loved and had longed so. Old associations, familiar faces, glances of recognition, smiles instead of blank stares. Oh, lovely!'

'It's charming to have you, darling Cynthia,' said Anna.

Then they embraced again, and then they linked arms and started on one of the old walks up and down the terrace.

'And you have enjoyed yourself, Cynthia?'

'Immensely! That's the only word for it. And Lucius too has quite fallen in love with travel. Still, now we are home, we shall stay here. I was just wondering how I have borne to stay away so long. It was so beautiful last night, so unutterably peaceful.

After dinner we came out here into the moonlight, and now and then we could hear the bells. Then I made Lucius stand against the window while I sang "Home, sweet Home" in the drawing-room. I'm sure he felt it was a melting moment.' She finished with the old joyous laugh.

'Oh, you must have had many a one whilst you've been away!'

'What, melting moments? I have. But at first I could not get Lucius, when he was melted, to stay melted. "Yes, yes, very fine, beautiful, charming," he would say, and the impression would pass instantly. While I could have gazed and gazed and gazed! He declared he only took me into the Himalayas and the Rockies because I was so transcendental. Oh, Anna, you must come and see the aloe, it's blossoming this year. Isn't it nice of it? And there are some lovely spikes of flowers on the yuccas. I think it's magic that is making all so perfect. What a happy soul am I! As for the rooms, you won't know them after the cases are unpacked. We've been busy with one already, but Lucius was called away. He is going to do all the business, you know. He'll be back soon, and then you shall make acquaintance at last. By the bye, how is Mrs. Severn, really well? Mr. Severn just answered in the ordinary way.'

'She is quite well,' said Anna. 'Far better than I thought she would have been.'

Cynthia nodded. If a shade crossed her face Anna was not allowed to see it.

'And you, dear? And Mr. Borlase, but oh! I need not ask. I saw him last night and thought he had never looked better. And you are still staunch friends, only waiting for some good reason of your own—perhaps for Antoinette to be useful. It's all right, you see.'

'Yes,' said Anna. 'And always will be between Geoff and me.'

They had gone round to the greenhouses, which stood on a slope in the full glow of the southern sun. As they passed down between the dazzling rows of begonias and fuchsias that were backed with ferns and exotics, Cynthia touched a flower here and there, burying her face in many a mass of bloom, and laughingly submitting to Anna's dusting off of the pollen afterwards.

'How old were you when you left Jersey and came to Old Lafer, Anna?' she said with apparent carelessness, after they had admired the aloe in its tub just outside the door.

'Ten, I believe,' said Anna. 'I was much younger than Clothilde, you know. She was my very much elder sister.'

'Half-sister, only that?' said Cynthia. 'Do you remember much of your life at Rocozanne?'

'I remember it chiefly because I still go there. I remember running about in the churchyard and playing with the gravedigger's dog. But we were not much there, you know, except in the holidays, until the year she was married. Ambrose Piton, my cousin, is to be married soon, and I am going to Rocozanne again almost immediately.'

'And did you always cross alone, and from Southampton.'

'I thought it was from Weymouth, the time we met Dad——'

'No, Southampton,' said Cynthia firmly. 'But never mind about the port. Was any one else ever with you? Did any one come to see you off? Do you remember any one assisting you? Did you always travel alone?'

Anna looked at her in astonishment.

'What questions!' she said. 'I fear I can't remember anything certainly. But I sometimes have an impression of some one looking after Clothilde and talking of India. But Clothilde always had friends. She was always beautiful, as you may imagine, and it seemed to be the height of felicity for any one to assist her. It's different when I go. But I am fortunately an independent person and able to manage for myself.'

'And supposing your memory is correct so far; do you remember in the least what——'

She stopped breathless. A rush of colour had suffused her face and neck, deepening the light of her eyes. She put her hand on Anna's arm, looking closely at her, and as though it hurt her to speak.

But at that moment a white setter rushed across the bowling-green and dashed up the path where they stood. Anna saw by the lightened change in Cynthia's face that Danby must be following.

They went on to meet him. He was slightly stouter than he had been when Cynthia first knew him, and looked broader in his rough light knickerbockers and loose jacket than he was naturally. But he was tall and well proportioned. His skin was at last tanned, Atlantic breezes had accomplished what Indian suns never had. Close shaving still produced an indigo tint on the jaw. His eyes, though still sardonic, had a suspicion of humour in their keenness. And his smile was pleasant.

Anna bowed and shook hands in perfect unconsciousness of ever having seen him before.

Cynthia watched her closely. So did Danby, though confident that there would be no recognition. He would not have known her. But then he had never paid much attention to her. Clothilde Hugo was not a woman to whom advance-guards and entrenchments were necessary on a lover's part. She was always ready to appropriate attraction to herself. To both, Anna had often been a tiresome inconvenience.

They all walked about the gardens some time longer before going in to lunch. Then they did some more unpacking. But conversation was on general topics; Anna forgot, indeed, that it had been personal earlier. Cynthia wanted to see as much of her to-day as possible. Her time would soon be occupied with town and county visits, to be followed by the shooting season.

When at last she left, they walked with her across the park to the woods. There Danby leant against the stile, while Cynthia and Anna finished their talk. He was lighting a cigarette. As he threw away the lucifer he happened to glance into the vista of the path which could be seen winding among the trees for some distance. But the glance was instantly mesmerised into concentration, for it lit on a figure in black. The figure was advancing half-way up the path, but it turned suddenly and instantly vanished. Danby had recognised it as the same he had seen in the Minster porch.

'Mrs. Severn,' he said to himself.

'Lucius,' said Cynthia, as they went slowly back, 'what a stupid brute that white setter is! He must be taught the value of times and seasons in polite society. I was just going to tell Anna Hugo something when he rushed at us. I was going to tell her how and when she had seen you before. I have made up my mind that I will.'

'If you have made up your mind I have nothing to say. You must have thought about it a good deal,' said Danby. He took the cigarette from his mouth and knocked off the ash.

'I have. You see Mrs. Severn must know you. She will call upon me, because if she didn't of her own will, Mr. Severn would require her to. She used sometimes to dine with us in grandmamma's time, she and Anna. She was an acquisition, very handsome and so musical. Mr. Severn would not understand our not amalgamating still. And I shall have to take you over to Old

Lafer for the same reason. And from what Mrs. Hennifer once said of her character I fancy it might turn out rather eccentric in some ways. Thus, as a safeguard, Anna had better know as much as Mrs. Severn herself. In fact she's going to Rocozanne, and it would be a marvel if that dear, gnome-like, gossiping Mr. Piton did not name your call.'

'He and Ambrose may think it undesirable that she should know; and besides that was two years ago, Cynthy.'

'Two? Dear me, so it was! But that won't matter when of course she'll talk about us—you and me, I mean. He would be sure to slip it out; besides, he'll be sure she will know by now. Yes, Lucius, I am convinced I ought to tell her. And I don't care. Every one may know, for what I care.'

'I fear social prejudice would then be certain you had "demeaned yourself." I fancied it had suspicions before we were married,' said Danby with more lightness than he just then felt.

'Social prejudice is a contemptible phantom,' said Cynthia with a curl of her lips. 'It's like a volcanic region. There are innumerable little cracks and fissures all over it, and you scarcely dare put a foot down lest the edges should crumble and precipitate you into fire. I thought of that at Honolulu.'

'Have you made memos of all your thoughts in their localities?'

'No. But really, Lucius, don't be so absurd. And let us discuss this matter seriously.'

'I didn't know you wanted to discuss. But it can still only lead to the fact of doing as you like. If I meet Mrs. Severn I shall raise my hat and walk on.'

'I know that. But the vital question is, what will she do?'

'Yes, it is, I grant,' said Danby.

'You do? Well, that must mean you think she might wish to do more than bow?'

'Granted again. I'm sorry to sear her with hot irons. But there are a lot of lonely places about here where we might unexpectedly come across each other, and she might speak to me and forfeit the remnant of good opinion I have for her. Have you any idea what she is doing now, Cynthia—I mean in the matter of respectable habits? You remember the old poacher's stigma?'

'Yes, I do. But I have not the least idea. I wish I had. But it is exactly what I cannot ask. Anna spoke of her to-day as being quite well. One thinks had Hartas been right, she must have undermined her health.'

'One does,' said Danby. He was still debating whether he should confess to having seen her that very hour, and so near that he felt he might at any time, in simply crossing the park, see her again.

'How far is it through that wood to Old Lafer, Cynthy?' he said.

'How far? I scarcely know, and I never thought of it. It will be in the Ordnance Survey. We'll look. The ground goes up and down. At first we see the path a long way, then there's a deep hollow; then we round the hill into the gill, and then there's a long way by the stream before we see the house against the moors.'

'Two miles, perhaps?'

'Oh, quite.'

'Does she ever come into the park as Miss Hugo does?'

'Never. It's private and too near the house on that side. Of course she might come if she chose. Mr. Severn walks constantly to the office. But I have never known her do it. She always drove round by East Lafer and the lanes when she called on granny. Anna is a friend of mine.'

They had reached the bowling-green again, and sat down on a seat in the shadow of the cedars before Danby had made up his

Lafer for the same reason. And from what Mrs. Hennifer once said of her character I fancy it might turn out rather eccentric in some ways. Thus, as a safeguard, Anna had better know as much as Mrs. Severn herself. In fact she's going to Rocozanne, and it would be a marvel if that dear, gnome-like, gossiping Mr. Piton did not name your call.'

'He and Ambrose may think it undesirable that she should know; and besides that was two years ago, Cynthy.'

'Two? Dear me, so it was! But that won't matter when of course she'll talk about us—you and me, I mean. He would be sure to slip it out; besides, he'll be sure she will know by now. Yes, Lucius, I am convinced I ought to tell her. And I don't care. Every one may know, for what I care.'

'I fear social prejudice would then be certain you had "demeaned yourself." I fancied it had suspicions before we were married,' said Danby with more lightness than he just then felt.

'Social prejudice is a contemptible phantom,' said Cynthia with a curl of her lips. 'It's like a volcanic region. There are innumerable little cracks and fissures all over it, and you scarcely dare put a foot down lest the edges should crumble and precipitate you into fire. I thought of that at Honolulu.'

'Have you made memos of all your thoughts in their localities?'

'No. But really, Lucius, don't be so absurd. And let us discuss this matter seriously.'

'I didn't know you wanted to discuss. But it can still only lead to the fact of doing as you like. If I meet Mrs. Severn I shall raise my hat and walk on.'

'I know that. But the vital question is, what will she do?'

'Yes, it is, I grant,' said Danby.

'You do? Well, that must mean you think she might wish to do more than bow?'

mind whether to say more. He flung one leg over the other knee and nursed it musingly. But as he often mused Cynthia thought nothing of this. She was prodding the grass with the end of her parasol.

They sat thus until the first dressing-bell rang. Danby started and pulled out his watch. Neither of them knew how the time had flown, or could conceive where it had gone.

Cynthia got up, and was on the terrace when he called her back.

'Well?' she said, having returned rather reluctantly.

'Sit down again; if the fish is spoiled it will only be like Frisco one day. Do you remember? Cynthy, I shall always tell you when by chance I run up against Mrs. Severn.'

'Of course you will. I shall always tell you, Lucius.'

He smiled, and she perceived the difference in the significance.

'I meant that of course you will always tell me everything.'

'And you, me.'

'I shall never have anything to tell.'

'My dear Cynthia!'

'I am quite a different woman to Mrs. Severn.'

'But, Cynthy, I don't expect to have to tell you any evil. My hope and meaning was that we should always simply exchange the day's events, incidents rather.'

'Well, I shall particularly like to know when you meet her, and what she says and does. That was my meaning, Lucius.'

She got up and turned away again with a smile. This time he did not call her back. If he did he would not tell her now. Not only had she surprised him by the construction she had put upon his words, but he was convinced it was pointed with jealousy. He could not think her knowingly jealous, he knew her too well, but certainly she was instinctively so. He felt that by his hesitation he had added importance to the accidental encounter of his glance with Mrs. Severn's. He ought to have pointed her out or named it instantly. He wished now that he had, while Anna was there. She might have innocently insisted upon calling her back. The meeting, taking place so naturally and before his wife, would have contained no elements of danger or sentimentality. He could have acted in such a manner as to convince her that no future one would either. Besides which, Anna's surprise would have compelled Mrs. Severn to tell her herself all the derogatory details.

Yes, he had made a mistake. To make good his own words too, he must never tell her this. He must begin to do so from the next encounter. He mused all along the terrace, feeling dissatisfied with himself. And yet if she were jealous, though only instinctively, it would probably have made her miserable to think Mrs. Severn had been so near the Hall, and might be again. He also had an uncomfortable suspicion that she had been there on the chance of seeing them. It was quite possible that she had calculated on the probability of their setting Anna across the park, where one or two of the Scotch cattle were not quite trustworthy. It would have been intolerable that Cynthia should be haunted by the possibility of her deliberately throwing herself in his way from the very first day of their return. Nevertheless he began to fear complications. Mrs. Hennifer might be right, she had known her many years, and to such a woman a tendency to one vice would be a fatal incentive to further self-indulgence. He determined that he would take the first opportunity Cynthia offered by reverting to the subject herself, to agree that Miss Hugo should know.

END OF VOL. II

Printed by R. & R. CLARK, *Edinburgh*

G. C. & Co

"One can never help enjoying 'Temple Bar.'"— *Guardian.*

Monthly at all Booksellers and Newsagents, price 1s.

"Who does not welcome 'Temple Bar.'"— *John Bull.*

"'TEMPLE BAR' is sparkling and brilliant. It might command a constituency by its fiction alone, but it takes so much care of its more solid matter that, if there were no stories at all, there is enough to interest the reader."—*English Independent.*

"A Magazine for the Million."—*Standard.*

RICHARD BENTLEY & SON, NEW BURLINGTON ST., LONDON.

One can never help enjoying **TEMPLE BAR**.—*Guardian.*

Monthly at all Booksellers and Newsagents, price 1s.

The Temple Bar Magazine.

Who does not welcome **TEMPLE BAR?**—*John Bull.*

PRICE ONE SHILLING.

TEMPLE BAR is always good.—*St. Stephen's Review.*

TEMPLE BAR is exceedingly readable.—*Society.*

TEMPLE BAR has capital contributions, fiction, fact, and fancy.—*The World.*

TEMPLE BAR continues to sustain the high prestige which belongs to it.—*County Gentleman.*

TEMPLE BAR contains Biographical Notices.

TEMPLE BAR contains short stories complete in each number.

The ever-welcome story-tellers of **TEMPLE BAR**.—*Jewish World.*

TEMPLE BAR very happily unites the best contents of the magazine as it was known and flourished a decade and more since with the features which readers demand in the modern review. The result is very happy.—*Sporting and Dramatic.*

TEMPLE BAR is invariably good. It is renowned for its high-class fiction.—*Bolton Guardian.*

TEMPLE BAR is the most readable of magazines.—*Pall Mall Gazette.*

TEMPLE BAR is of all English magazines the one which most cunningly blends fiction with fact.—*Figaro.*

TEMPLE BAR is as good as usual. Few keep their level more equally.—*Spectator,* July 11, 1885.

TEMPLE BAR'S Biographical Papers are always interesting.—*Glasgow Herald.*

TEMPLE BAR contains Literary Articles.

Essays of the **TEMPLE BAR** type, solid yet vivacious, not too learned, but not too superficial.—*Manchester Examiner.*

TEMPLE BAR contains Historical Reviews.

TEMPLE BAR has a well-established fame for admirable Historical Articles.—*Western Daily Mercury.*

TEMPLE BAR has articles on French Literature.

French Literature and Literary Characters are always welcome in **TEMPLE BAR**.—*Morning Post.*

TEMPLE BAR is as good as ever, and that is saying a good deal.—*Lady's Pictorial.*

TEMPLE BAR is sparkling and brilliant. It might command a constituency by its fiction alone, but it takes so much care of its more solid matter that, if there were no stories at all, there is enough to interest the reader.—*English Independent.*

A Magazine for the Million.—*Standard.*

RICHARD BENTLEY & SON, NEW BURLINGTON ST., LONDON.

www.ingramcontent.com/pod-product-compliance
Lightning Source LLC
Chambersburg PA
CBHW032104230426
43672CB00009B/1631